W9-DDR-609

From a
Monastery Kitchen

From a Monastery Kitchen

REVISED EDITION

Brother Victor-Antoine d'Avila-Latourrette

HARPER AND ROW, PUBLISHERS

FROM A MONASTERY KITCHEN, Revised Edition.
Copyright ©1989 by Victor-Antoine d'Avila-Latourrette.
Preface to the Revised Edition and Introduction copyright © 1989.
by Elise Boulding.

All rights reserved. Printed in the United States of America. No part
of this book may be used or reproduced in any manner whatsoever
without written permission except in the case of brief quotations
embodied in critical articles and reviews. For information address
Harper & Row, Publishers, Inc., 10 East 53 Street, New York, NY
10022. Published simultaneously in Canada by Fitzhenry & Whiteside,
Limited, Toronto.

Produced by Wieser & Wieser
118 East 25th Street, New York, NY 10010

FIRST EDITION

Library of Congress Cataloging in Publication Data

D'Avila-Latourrette, Victor-Antoine.
   From a monastery kitchen.

   Rev. Ed. of: From a monastery kitchen/Elise
Boulding. 1st ed. c1976.
Includes index.
   1. Vegetarian cookery. 2. Monastic and religious life. 3. Quotations,
English. I. Boulding, Elise. I. From a monastery kitchen. II. Title.
TX837.D25 1989   641.5'636   88-45997
ISBN 0-06-250037-6   1.5636

89 90 91 92 93   10 9 8 7 6 5 4 3 2 1

Photography in FROM A MONASTERY KITCHEN *is the work of George G.
Wieser, Jr., Albert Poelzl, and the Reverend Patrick Mooney. Credits
for photographs are as follows:*
GEORGE G. WIESER, JR.: *front cover center and right; back cover top left
and right, lower left, center and right; and page 65.*
ALBERT POELZL: *front cover left; back cover top center; and page 11.*
REVEREND PATRICK MOONEY: *page 39 and page 95.*

Contents

Summer

Autumn

DESSERTS

The Basics

Preface to the Revised Edition

I have just re-read the Introduction to *From a Monastery Kitchen* that I wrote in 1976. I have had to read it in the Dutch translation, since I have only one Dutch and one Japanese copy of the cookbook left; no English copy in my library! It has brought a warm rush of memories of the time when Brother Victor, Sister Jeanne-Marie, Sister Donald and others gathered with me at Our Lady of the Resurrection Monastery to pray together and to work on that first monastic cookbook. We continue to be close although we see each other less often. Our Lady of the Resurrection has moved further up the Hudson to a setting of great beauty. Sister Jean-Marie and Sister Donald now have their own monastic center, the Sisters of the Transfiguration, in the rolling hills of upstate New York. The family life of each monastery, as a model for family life everywhere, continues to bless all who come there. Body and spirit are nourished by kitchen and chapel. The rhythm of monastic life, framed by morning and evening holy office, continues to form the basic pattern of life. It is my joy, although I live "In the world" and have less time in my own Colorado hermitage than I would like, to participate in spirit in that monastic rhythm, and to remember continually that the kitchen table too is an altar.

I am very happy that Brother Victor has been inspired to write down new recipes so that a new cookbook is now available carrying the same spirit as the old one, but in a different format. *From a Monastery Kitchen* graced kitchens in many lands, and I know it will continue to do so.

Welcome to the holy kitchen of the extended monastic family!

--Elise Boulding
Boulder, Colorado
November 28, 1988

Introduction

When our five children were small, some years ago, my morning trip to deliver them to their respective schools took us each day past a local monastery just at the hour when the monks were about in the garden. A few walked with heads bowed; others read their prayer books. The deep silence in the garden somehow penetrated our noisy car, and I never passed that spot without feeling joy.

A few years ago, while seeking a place to quiet retreat between conferences in New York City, I was led to Our Lady of the Resurrection Priory, then in Cold Spring, for a weekend of prayer. Many times since then I have journeyed up the Hudson River on the bumpy Poughkeepsie local to enter the life of prayer that Brother Victor-Antoine generously shares with those who come to the farmhouse monastery.

During the first visit I discovered something: monasteries have kitchens, and monks have to cook. I had read about Brother Lawrence, the illiterate lay brother who practiced the presence of God in a monastery kitchen in 17th century Europe, but I didn't know that the monks continued his practice in twentieth-century kitchens. Not only do monks have to cook, they have to wash dishes and do every kind of houskeeping chore. While they do not usually have young children to feed, they have many guests and must always be ready to set an extra place at the refectory table. As I visited other monasteries, I became aware of how hard our comtemplative brothers and sisters work. Besides household chores, they farm and do craft work and make bread, cheese, or other items to sell. They work as hard as those of us "on the outside" because they too must make ends meet. Monasteries are largely self supporting.

Since our contemplative brothers and sisters are vowed to a life of poverty, their kitchen work is often hard. Monasteries grow much of their own food, and young monks learn the art of food preservation. There are monks who are gifted cooks, like Brother Victor-Antoine, whose delicious simple meals, served in a spirit of deepest prayer, inspired the idea for this book. At Our Lady of the Resurrection Monastery, this gift for cooking is combined with a gift for frugality that chooses discarded food from supermarket trash bins and lovingly renders society's leavings edible. Brother Victor-Antoine also has a gift of song, and when he is not in the kitchen, he is sitting at a work table writing and arranging music for the daily hours of prayer (divine office) in the chapel and for graces sung before meals. Praying, working, cooking, eating, singing, silence, and frugality--all these come together in the sacrament of the refectory.

Many of our monastic brothers and sisters come from farmer stock, like the rest of us, and monastery kitchens reflect the same double feast of body and spirit that the surrounding communities enjoy. Feast days, in fact, probably have always meant more in monasteries than anywhere else because of the sheer contrast with the disciplined asceticism of daily life. A monastic feast day is sober enough at that, but special foods are cooked with such care, special songs sung with such exaltation, that the whole monastery vibrates with holy joy. Holy feasting is not just a safety valve, however; it is a deep reaffirmation of the fact of Incarnation. The Son of Man came eating and drinking.

The cloister *is* very different from the outside world. If it were not, those of us who live in the world would not be drawn there. There is in the monastery a pointing of the whole life toward God, a drawing together of every activity into prayer. Again and again each day the monks return to the chapel, the very heart of every monastery, to lift up their hearts to God in silence, in word, and in song throughout the hours bounded by predawn vigils and evening prayers. These two offices, vigils and evening prayer, are like jeweled gates through which the monks move the world toward heaven every day of their lives.

This book was born in the kitchen of Our Lady of the Resurrection Priory. Having shared the joys of mealtime and even a little of the weariness of work with my monastic brothers and sisters, it came to me very strongly that this experience should and could be shared with other women and men. This book is intended to open the monastery door in a symbolic way for those who may never come here but who like to evoke the peace of the monastery in their own kitchens.

--Elise Boulding
Boulder, Colorado

How to Use This Cookbook

This is a vegetarian cookbook; no meat recipes are included, but there are fish recipes. Not all monastics are vegetarian by any means, but the rule of Saint Benedict, which Our Lady of the Resurrection Monastery follows, strongly encourages abstaining from meat. And each of us today must consider whether we want more than the least of us on the planet can have; most of our brothers and sisters do not have meat. Frugality takes many forms, and the way of simplicity that is most appropriate for any one household will be unique to that home.

If we were to reconstruct a typical monastic daily fare from the recipes that follow, it might be something like this: Breakfast would be simply coffee and one or two slices of bread. Lunch could include lentil and lemon peel soup, mixed fruit salad, puffed cheese toasts, and tea. A supper menu might include vegetable-cheese casserole, acorn squash, apple crumble, and tea.

The dinner table in a monastery is always set with care for both daily fare and feast days. Food is arranged to show the full beauty of God's harvest in vegetables, grains, dairy products, and fruit. Each night before the meal begins, the brothers or sisters of the order stand at their places around the candlelit table and sing grace. Then they quietly settle down to listening to the evening reading from Scripture or a classic religious writing while they eat. The delight in the fellowship of the table is always enhanced by one special ingredient added to every dish served: preparation with love.

The recipes that follow are arranged seasonally in order to link the great rhythms of human life: the seasons of the year, the seasons of the church, and the seasons of the heart. Within each season, recipes are grouped in the order in which they come at the meal, from soup to dessert.

Each recipe is accompanied by a quotation and art that is intended to reflect the nearly two-thousand-year-old experience of monastic life as an affirmation of wholeness, simplicity, and joy. Some quotations are directly about monastic life; others represent the same spirit of affirmation from secular life.

Many monasteries sell locally the food products they make, such as bread, cheese, and jellies. Contemplative monasteries are strung like rosary beads all across North America, as they are also on every continent. You may wish to seek out the one nearest you, not only to inquire whether it sells food, but to experience, in the monastery chapel, the grace and joy that is generated in the twentieth-century centers of contemplative life.

WINTER

Blessed is the season which engages the whole world in a conspiracy of love.

—*Hamilton W. Mabie*

Soups

Hermit's Soup

Solitude, prayer, love, and abstinence are the four wheels of the vehicle that carries our spirit heavenward.

—*St. Seraphim of Sarov*

1 turnip
2 carrots
1 small cabbage
1 onion
  oil
1/3 cup rice
8 cups water
  salt to taste

Wash and trim the vegetables. Slice thinly.

Sauté vegetables for a few minutes in oil in a soup kettle. Add the rice and 2 quarts of water, stir well, cover the pan, and simmer slowly for 1 hour. Add the salt just before serving.

1–2 servings

Potato Soup

Consider your call, brothers and sisters; not many of you were wise according to worldly standards, not many were powerful, not many were of noble birth; but God chose what is foolish in the world to shame the wise, God chose what is weak in the world to shame the strong . . . so that no human being might boast in the presence of God. God is the source of your life.

—I Corinthians:26-30

4 tablespoons butter
1 onion, finely minced
2 quarts milk
4 cups mashed potatoes
2 tablespoons flour
4 tablespoons chopped parsley
salt and pepper to taste

Melt the butter in a skillet and gently sauté the onion, without browning, until soft.

Transfer the onion to the top of a double boiler. Add the milk and the potatoes. Stir thoroughly with a wire whip or mixer until smooth. Add seasoning and heat slowly over hot water until soup almost comes to a boil. Reduce the heat and simmer for 10 minutes. Add salt and pepper to taste; sprinkle with parsley and serve.

8 servings

Saint Nicholas Soup
(Potage Saint-Nicholas)

Saint Nicholas, a bishop of Myra in the 4th century, is one of the best loved saints in both the Eastern and Western churches. He was the original "Santa Claus' and in many countries of Europe, presents were exchanged on December 6, his feast day. From Europe the lovely custom of giving gifts during the Christmas season came to America. Because his feast usually falls within the first week of Advent, he is considered an Advent saint who joyfully points toward the coming of the Lord. Today, in some European monasteries, his feast is celebrated with revivals of medieval plays about his life.

2 leeks or onions
5 medium carrots
2 turnips
5 potatoes
1/2 medium cabbage
4 tablespoons butter
1 teaspoon salt (or more, according to taste)
4 quarts water
1/3 cup minced chervil
   croutons

Peel and dice the vegetables. Shred the cabbage.

Melt the butter in a large soup pot. Add the vegetables, salt, and stir. Turn off the heat, cover the pot, and let it rest for 15 to 20 minutes.

Add the water and bring the soup to a boil. Reduce the heat to low to medium, cover the pot, and cook slowly for 30 to 40 minutes. Stir from time to time.

When the soup is done, puree in a blender until it is creamy and smooth. Serve hot, garnished with croutons and chervil.

6–8 servings

Chickpea Soup

In the midst of winter, I realized that deep within me was an invincible summer.

—Albert Camus

2 cups chickpeas
2 cups canned tomatoes
1 large onion, chopped
1 stalk celery, minced
2 carrots, sliced
4 garlic cloves, minced
1 red pepper, diced
4 tablespoons olive oil
1 bouillon cube
1 bay leaf
   salt and pepper to taste

Soak chickpeas overnight. Cover with water and bring to a boil. Add all remaining ingredients and cook slowly over medium heat for about 1 hour until the peas and all of the vegetables are tender. Adjust seasoning. Cover and simmer the soup for about 15 minutes. Serve hot.

6-8 servings

Saint Anthony of the Desert Soup

Saint Anthony, called the Great, lived in Egypt between 251 and 356 A.D. At age 18, the Gospel text: "If you wish to be perfect, go and sell all that you have and then follow me," so moved him that he left everything behind and retired to an inaccessible place in the wilderness where he dedicated his life to God in manual work and continual prayer. In his old age, he imparted wisdom to his disciples and encouraged them to lead a monastic life. Because he was the first Christian to retire to a monastic life, he is considered to be the first monk and also the father of all monks. His feast is celebrated on January 17.

1 cup barley
1 carrot, finely grated
2 leeks, sliced
1 bay leaf
1/3 cup fresh parsley, minced
3 tablespoons oil
  salt to taste
7 cups water
1 bouillon cube and chopped
  mushrooms, if desired

Heat the oil in a soup pan and add the barley, stirring continuously for one minute. Immediately add the carrot, leeks, bay leaf, parsley, salt, and 7 cups of water.

Cook the soup over low/medium heat for 40 to 45 minutes until the barley is tender. Add more water if needed. For extra taste, add the bouillon and the mushrooms during last 20 minutes of simmering. Serve hot.

4 servings

Main Dishes
Red Beans in Wine
(Haricots rouges au vin)

Our hope is that the winter of humanity will gradually be transformed to the bursting forth of love, for it is to this that we are called.

—*Jean Vanier*

4 cups dry red beans
6 tablespoons butter
4 onions, sliced
1 tablespoon flour
1 bottle of red wine
  salt and pepper to taste

Soak the beans overnight. Cook the beans in salted water for about 1 1/2 to 2 hours until they are tender. Drain.

Melt the butter in a saucepan, and lightly brown the onions, then remove with slotted spoon. Add the flour, and stir to make roux. Add the wine slowly, continuing to stir until the mixture is a smooth sauce. Add the beans and onions, and simmer, covered, for 30 minutes, stirring from time to time so beans on bottom do not burn. Serve hot with rice, fish, or eggs.

6 servings

Leeks au Gratin
(Poireaux au Gratin)

Saint Anthony the Great said: "When I was visiting an abbot, a virgin came and said to the old man, 'Abba, I spend my life fasting; I eat once a week and study the Old and New Testaments every day.' The old man answered, 'Have poverty and plenty become a matter of indifference to you?' 'No,' she said. 'Disgrace and praise?' 'No,' she said. 'Enemies and friends?' 'No,' she said. Then the wise old man said, 'Go and work, you have achieved nothing.' "

—letter from a Russian monk

12 leeks
 1 cup grated Gruyère cheese
   (or similar cheese)
   butter
   salt and pepper

white sauce
 4 tablespoons butter
 4 tablespoons flour
 2 cups milk

Preheat oven to 350°.

Select fresh leeks. Wash and clean them well, trimming them off at the top, where the leaves begin to get hard. Cook them in boiling salted water for 30 minutes. Rinse and drain them thoroughly.

Butter an oblong baking dish and cover the entire bottom with 1 cup white sauce. Attractively arrange the leeks in the dish and cover them with the rest of the white sauce. Sprinkle the surface of the dish with the grated Gruyère cheese. Bake at 350° for 25 to 30 minutes.

4–6 servings

Stuffed Acorn Squash

Idleness is an enemy of the soul. Therefore the brethren should be occupied at certain times in manual labor, and at other times in sacred reading. For they are truly monks when they live by the labor of their hands, as did our fathers and the apostles.

—from the Holy Rule of St. Benedict

3 medium acorn squashes
  olive oil
1 large onion, chopped
3 garlic cloves, finley minced
6 tablespoons parsley, minced
6 mushrooms, finely chopped
1 egg
1/3 cup milk
1 cup bread crumbs
  salt and pepper to taste
  grated cheese of your choice

Preheat oven to 350°. Wash and rinse the squash. Cut in half and remove seeds. Fill a large saucepan with water and bring to boil. Place the squash in the pan, cut side down and boil for 8 to 10 minutes. Drain immediately.

Heat sufficient amount of oil in a large skillet and sauté the onion, garlic, parsley and mushrooms for a few minutes, stirring continuously.

In a deep bowl beat the egg and milk together. Add the vegetable mixture and bread crumbs. Mix all very well and season to taste.

Butter a flat baking dish and arrange the acorn squash halves in it. Divide the vegetable mixture evenly among the squash halves, filling the cavities. Sprinkle with grated cheese and add 1 teaspoon of oil to the center of each squash half. Bake in a preheated oven at 350° for 20 to 25 minutes. Serve hot.

6 servings

Saint Stephen's Scrambled Eggs
(Oeufs brouillés Saint-Étienne)

Saint Stephen is considered a Christmas saint because his feast is celebrated the day after Christmas, the 26th of December. St. Stephen, "a man full of faith and power," was one of the first seven deacons of the early Church, chosen by the Apostles to look after the needs of the poor, the orphans and widows. He is considered to be the Church's first martyr. While still a young man, he was stoned to death outside the city of Jerusalem for confessing his faith in the Lord Jesus.

6 tomatoes
  oil
6 eggs
6 tablespoons heavy cream
  salt and pepper to taste
4 tablespoons butter
6 large onions, sliced

Preheat oven to 250°.

Choose 6 large, firm tomatoes, and slice off the top part of each. Scoop out the insides being careful to leave the shells intact. Heat a few tablespoons of oil in a large skillet and with care cook the tomatoes for 1 or 2 minutes, first with the cut-side down so that the water from the tomatoes evaporates. Turn the tomatoes carefully, and cook the other side also for 2 minutes. The tomatoes must remain firm. Place the tomato shells in a greased baking dish and keep them warm in a 250° oven.

Beat the eggs and heavy cream thoroughly. Add salt and pepper, and beat some more. Melt the butter in a large skillet and scramble the eggs. When the eggs are done (there must be some moisture left in them), fill the tomato shells with the eggs and place them back in the oven to keep warm.

Pour several tablespoons of oil into the skillet and gently fry the onions until they turn brown. Place the onions in a round serving dish and arrange the 6 tomatoes in the center. Serve hot.

6 servings

Tuna Stuffed Peppers

It is not necessary to fear our weakness. . . . The most necessary things to fear are devilish pride, vainglory, hostility and condemnation, but weaknesses serve to humble our imagined piety.

—*letter from a Russian monk*

4 green peppers
1 egg, slightly beaten
1/3 cup heavy cream
6 ounces canned tuna fish, flaked
1/2 cup bread crumbs
1 onion, chopped
1/2 cup chopped and minced parsley
1 tablespoon mustard
salt and pepper to taste
grated cheese of your choice

Preheat oven to 350°.

Choose large fresh peppers and boil them whole for about 5 minutes. Drain carefully and allow to cool. Cut the peppers in half and remove the seeds.

In a deep bowl, beat the egg and the cream together. Add remaining ingredients, except the grated cheese, and mix thoroughly.

Butter a baking dish and fill the pepper halves with the tuna mixture. Bake at 350° for about 20 minutes. Sprinkle the tops with the grated cheese and bake for another 5 minutes until the cheese melts. Serve hot.

4 servings

Lentils and Rice Loaf
(the vegetarian equivalent of meat loaf)

See yonder stars so bright and clear
That praise their Maker as they move
And usher in the circling year.

—*Schiller*

1 cup lentils
1 cup rice
  olive oil
1 large onion, sliced
2 tomatoes, chopped
10 mushrooms, sliced
2 garlic cloves, minced
1 green pepper, diced
3 tablespoons minced parsley
1 teaspoon thyme
2 eggs
1/3 cup milk
1/2 cup bread crumbs

Preheat oven to 350°.

Wash and rinse the lentils. Add the lentils, rice, and 2 tablespoons of oil to 4 cups water in a heavy saucepan. Cook over medium heat until they are well done and all water evaporates. (If brown rice is used, you may need more water.)

In a large skillet heat 4 tablespoons olive oil and gently saute the sliced onions, tomatoes, mushrooms, minced garlic, and green pepper until they turn golden. Add the parsley and thyme and stir for 1 or 2 minutes.

Beat the eggs in a large bowl. Add the milk, bread crumbs, salt and pepper, and beat some more. Add the cooked lentils, rice, and sautéed vegetables to the egg mixture. Mix everything well and pour into a well-greased bread pan and bake at 350° for 40 to 50 minutes. The loaf is done when all liquid has evaporated. Serve hot.

NOTE: You may wish to sauté extra vegetables and serve them as an accompaniment to the loaf.

4–6 servings

Potato and Parsley Casserole

Fickleness and indecision are signs of self-love. If you can never make up your mind what God wills for you, but are always veering from one opinion to another, . . . from one method to another, it may be an indication that you are trying to get around God's will and do your own with a quiet conscience. So keep still, and let God do some work.

—*Thomas Merton*

4 garlic cloves, minced
6 tablespoons vegetable oil
8 potatoes, sliced
1 large onion, sliced
1/2 cup finely chopped parsley
  salt and pepper to taste
  butter

Preheat oven to 350°.

Thoroughly butter a 2-quart casserole dish. Briefly sauté the minced garlic in the oil and cover the bottom of the casserole dish with it.

Fill the casserole with layers as follows: sliced potatoes, onions, parsley, salt and pepper. Repeat layers. Season and dot top with butter.

At the edge (so as not to wash off seasonings,) add enough water to cover 2/3 to 3/4 of the potatoes. Place a lid on the casserole and bake at 350° for about 1 hour, removing the lid for the last 15 minutes.

6–8 servings

Subiaco Fish Fillets

Mount Subiaco is the holy mountain south of Rome where Saint Benedict retired to live as a hermit at the beginning of his monastic life. At the small monastery still there on the site, the monks joyfully continue to follow in the footsteps of St. Benedict. The monastery attracts many visitors year-round who come not only to venerate the memory of the Patriarch of the West, but also to see the beautiful medieval frescoes in the monastic church.

1 1/2 cups homemade tomato sauce
(see The Basics section)
4 fillets of firm fish
1 egg, slightly beaten
1/2 cup flour
salt and pepper to taste
2 tablespons butter
4 tablespoons olive oil
olives, parsley sprigs, lemon
slices for garnish

Prepare a good tomato sauce following your favorite recipe and keep it hot.

Dip the fish fillets in egg, then in flour seasoned with salt and pepper.

Heat butter and oil in a heavy frying pan and fry the fillets gently for 10 to 15 minutes, depending on their thickness, turning as necessary.

Arrange the fillets on a serving platter and place the garnish around them. Spoon some sauce on top of each fillet, and serve the rest in a gravy boat.

4 servings

Cabbage and Apples Béarnaise Style

The monk must ever begin again and again, and whatever he does, he remains the unprofitable servant.

—*Mother Maria*

1 large cabbage
4 tablespoons sugar
1 teaspoon salt
1/2 cup cider vinegar
6 tablespoons vegetable oil
4 tablespoons butter
4 sour apples, peeled and cut into eighths
1/2 cup red wine
2 tablespoons lemon juice

Slice the head of cabbage as you would for cole slaw. Place in a saucepan with the sugar, salt, and cider vinegar. Stir, then cover the pan and let it stand for 30 minutes.

Add the butter and oil to the saucepan with the cabbage. Stir thoroughly. Place the apples on the top of the cabbage. Cover the saucepan and cook over low heat, simmering slowly.

As the cabbage cooks, add sufficient water to prevent scorching. Cook slowly for 1 hour 20 minutes. Add 1/2 cup red wine, lemon juice, and more salt if needed. Heat. The cabbage should be deliciously moist. Serve as an accompaniment to a main course.

6–8 servings

Corn Meal Mush
(Polenta)

The monks should wait on one another, and let no one be excused from the kitchen service, except by reason of sickness or occupation in some important work. For this service brings increase of reward and of charity.

—from the Holy Rule of St. Benedict

1 cup cold water
1 cup yellow corn meal
6 tablespoons vegetable oil
1 teaspoon salt
3 cups boiling water
1 cup chopped onion
2 garlic cloves, crushed
2 green peppers, finely chopped
4 tablespoons olive oil
3/4 teaspoon salt
1 pound canned tomatoes
1 6 ounce can tomato paste
1/2 teaspoon oregano
   dash pepper to taste
1 cup grated yellow cheese

Combine cold water, corn meal, oil, and salt. Stir to eliminate lumps. Add to the boiling water, stirring well. Return to boil, stirring constantly. Reduce heat, cover the pot. Cook for 10 minutes, stirring occasionally. Pour into a 10-inch greased ovenproof dish.

Sauté onion, garlic, and green peppers in the olive oil. Add salt, tomatoes, tomato paste, oregano, and dash of pepper. Cook, stirring frequently. Reduce heat and simmer for 30 minutes. Pour the sauce over the polenta and cover with grated cheese. Bake for about 30 minutes in a 350° oven until sauce is bubbly and cheese melted.

6–8 servings

Mimosa Salad
(Salade mimosa)

Whatever else be lost among the years,
Let us keep Christmas still a shining thing.

—*Grace N. Crowell*

2 heads bibb lettuce
2 heads Boston lettuce
2 Belgium endives
3 hard-boiled eggs, chopped

tarragon vinaigrette (see The Basics section)
8 tablespoons olive oil
2 tablespoons tarragon vinegar
1 tablespoon lemon juice
1 teaspoon French mustard
   (preferably tarragon mustard)
   salt and pepper

Wash and dry the lettuce and the endives thoroughly. Separate the leaves gently, and place them into a big salad bowl.

Just before serving, prepare the vinaigrette according to instructions in The Basics section. Pour it over the salad, and add the crumbled hard-boiled eggs. Toss the salad and serve.

8 servings

Broccoli and Tomato Salad

Except the Christ be born again tonight
In dreams of all men, saints and sons of shame,
The world will never see his kingdom bright.

—Vachel Lindsay

2 large heads fresh broccoli
4 ripe tomatoes
1 bunch arugula, or endives, or
   mesclun

vinaigrette (see The Basics
section)
8 tablespoons olive oil
2 tablespoons tarragon vinegar
2 tablespoons lemon juice
1 teaspoon French mustard
1 shallot, finely minced
   salt and pepper to taste

Soak the broccoli in water for one hour. Separate the broccoli florets from the stems. Slice the upper part of the stems thinly and discard the tough parts. Place the broccoli florets and the slices from the stems into a pot of salted boiling water. Boil for 5 to 7 minutes. Rinse the broccoli immediately after boiling in cold water so that the broccoli maintains its fresh green color.

Peel the tomatoes, if desired. Cut them in half and discard the pulp and seeds. Cut the tomatoes in thin slices.

Wash and dry the leafy greens and place with broccoli and tomatoes in a salad bowl. Prepare the vinaigrette according to instructions in The Basics section. Just before serving pour the vinaigrette over the salad. Toss the salad and serve.

6 servings

Desserts and Breads
Crêpes Saint-Gwenolé

The proof of love is in the works. Where love exists, it does great things. But where it ceases to act, it ceases to exist.

—*St. Gregory the Great*

3 eggs (for more tender crêpes, use only the yolks)
1 1/2 cups sifted flour
1 cup milk
1/2 cup water
4 tablespoons melted butter
2 tablespoons orange liqueur
1 tablespoon sugar
2 tablespoons grated orange rind
powdered sugar (superfine, not confectioners')

Beat the eggs. Gradually stir in flour, then milk, water, and melted butter. Batter must "rest," covered and in the refrigerator for at least 2 hours; overnight is fine.

Stir in orange liqueur, sugar, grated orange rind.

Select a small frying pan, preferably one with low sides, no more than 7 inches in diameter. Oil or butter it for each crêpe.

For each crêpe, pour about 3 tablespoons of batter into warm pan and rotate to spread batter evenly over surface. Batter should be very thin. (Trial and error will determine best heat or necessity to add a few tablespoons of milk to thin batter slightly, etc.) When one side of crêpe is golden, run spatula around edge of crêpe, then under it, and turn it to brown other side. As each crêpe is done, sprinkle powdered sugar on the surface and fold it in quarters. Stack and cover with waxed paper.

4 servings
(about 12 crêpes)

Pumpkin Pear Sauce

When you pray, shut your eyes for a moment and try to concentrate your spiritual powers. If you get tired, raise your eyes to the icon or the lighted candle. Concentrating on prayer this way, the heart will find within itself that spiritual warmth which comes from Christ himself and fills one's whole being with peace and joy.

—*St. Seraphim of Sarov*

10 pears or apples
1 small pumpkin
1/2 cup sugar (or more)
2 tablespoons grated orange rind
1 teaspoon vanilla extract
1 teaspoon cinnamon (optional)
  nutmeg to taste

Wash pears or apples, but do not peel. Cut into chunks and remove seeds. Peel the pumpkin, and remove the seeds and pith.

Place the pears or apples and pumpkin in a heavy kettle; add sugar, orange rind, vanilla, nutmeg, cinnamon, and water to cover these ingredients. Cover the pot and cook over low heat for an hour, stirring occasionally, until fruits are tender. Put through food grinder, ricer or blender, and chill. Serve very cold.

8 servings

Gaudete Date and Rice Pudding

For who hath naught to give but love,
Gives all his heart away,
And giving all, hath all to give,
Another Christmas Day.

—*Charles W. Kennedy*

1 cup rice
2 cups water
1 teaspoon salt
1 cup milk
1/3 cup brown sugar
1 egg, well beaten
1 cup chopped dates
1/2 cup raisins
2 tablespoons cognac
whipping cream
confectioners' sugar

Simmer the rice in salted water in a large saucepan until the rice is done.

In a separate saucepan, dissolve the sugar in the cup of milk. Add the well beaten egg, the chopped dates and raisins, and the cognac and cook over low heat for about 5 minutes, stirring continuously. Simmer for another 5 minutes. Combine this mixture and the rice in a deep bowl and fold together thoroughly. Divide the mixture into 4 dessert dishes and chill for at least 2 hours before serving.

Before serving, whip the cream with a mixer, slowly adding confectioners' sugar according to taste and one tablespoon of cognac. Top each dish with a good portion of whipped cream and serve cold.

4 servings

Cloister Molasses Apple Cake

The monastery should be so established that all the necessary things, such as water, mill, garden and various workshops may be within the enclosure so that there is no necessity for the monks to go outside of it, since that is not at all profitable for their souls.

—from the Holy Rule of St. Benedict

1 1/2 cups peeled and thinly sliced apples
3/4 cup molasses
1/3 cup margarine or shortening
1/2 cup hot water
2 1/2 cups flour
1/2 cup sugar
1 teaspoon cinnamon
1/2 teaspoon cloves
1/4 teaspoon nutmeg
1 tablespoon baking powder
1/4 teaspoon salt

Preheat oven to 350°.

Cook the apples in the molasses slowly until they are tender, stirring frequently to prevent scorching.

Melt the margarine or shortening in the hot water. Sift all dry ingredients, and gradually add the hot water mixture, stirring constantly to keep smooth. Stir in molasses and apple mixture.

Pour the entire mixture into a well-greased oblong 8 by 12-inch pan. Bake at 350° for about 30 minutes. Serve warm.

6–8 servings

Apple Compote

I have come to the conclusion that the most important element in human life is faith. If God were to take away all the blessings, health, physical fitness, wealth, intelligence, and leave me with but one gift, I would ask for faith—for with faith in God, in God's goodness, mercy, love for me, and belief in everlasting life, I believe I could still be happy, trustful, leaving all to God's inscrutable providence.

—Rose Kennedy

2 cups water
1/2 cups sugar (depending on sweetness of apples)
2 pounds apples (peeled, cored and cut in halves or quarters depending on size)
2 pieces lemon peel
5 whole cloves

Heat water and sugar together. When the sugar is completely dissolved, add apples, lemon peel, and cloves. Cook about 20 minutes over high heat. Chill and serve.

6 servings

Twelfth Night Cake

Happy, happy Christmas, that can take us back to the delusions of our childish days, that can recall to the old man the pleasures of his youth and transport the traveler, thousands of miles away, back to his own friends and his quiet home.

—*Charles Dickens*

1 cup shortening
2 2/3 cups sugar
5 1/2 cups flour
5 teaspoons baking powder
1/2 teaspoon salt
1 1/2 cups milk
6 egg whites, beaten
2 teaspoons vanilla extract

icing
2 cups confectioners' sugar
1/2 cup butter or margarine
2 tablespoons milk or cream

gumdrops

Preheat oven to 375°.

Cream shortening and sugar until fluffy. Sift dry ingredients together. Add milk alternately with the sifted dry ingredients to the creamed mixture.

Fold in beaten egg whites. Add vanilla and stir.

Divide batter evenly between three 9-inch greased layer cake pans and bake at 375° for about 30 minutes.

Prepare the icing by beating the ingredients together until stiff. Spread icing between layers and as a frosting. Decorate the top with a crown of gumdrops.

6–8 servings

Dutchess County Apple and Pear Tart

Blessed of the Lord be his land, for the precious thing of heaven, for the dew, and for the deep that croucheth beneath, and for the precious fruits brought forth by the sun.

—Deuteronomy 33:13

 3 cooking apples, thinly sliced
 3 cooking pears, thinly sliced
 6 tablespoons apple brandy
 2 tablespoons lemon juice
1/4 teaspoon nutmeg
 4 ounces apple jelly
 2 egg whites, stiffly beaten

pastry shell
2 cups flour
1 stick butter or margarine
  pinch of salt
1 egg or 2 egg yolks
5 tablespoons ice water

Prepare the pastry shell according to directions in The Basics section, using 2 egg yolks. Prebake at 350° for about 12 minutes.

Mix the fruit slices with the brandy, lemon juice and nutmeg.

Fill the pastry shell with an even apple and pear layer following the design of a revolving wheel. Cover the surface with half the apple jelly. Place another layer of fruit on the top of the first one. Cover with the rest of the apple jelly and top with the beaten egg whites. Bake at 350° for about 30 to 40 minutes. Let cool before serving.

NOTE: Dutchess County in New York State, home of Our Lady of the Resurrection, is rich agricultural land, well-known for the marvelous apples and pears it produces. The long rows of apple orchards across the county enhance the beauty of the rural landscape. Unfortunately, the pressure of development on local farmers is such that unless local officials protect the county's long tradition of agriculture, farms and orchards may soon be a thing of the past.

8 servings

Christmas Day Bread
(Christstollen)

As fits the holy Christmas birth.
Be this, good friend, our carols still—
Be peace on earth, be peace on earth,
To men of gentle will.

—*William M. Thackeray*

1 package cake yeast
1 tablespoon sugar
1/4 cup lukewarm water
1 cup shortening
1 1/4 cups sugar
2 eggs
2 cups lukewarm scalded milk
6 cups flour
1 teaspoon salt
1/2 teaspoon nutmeg
1 cup raisins
1 cup currants
1/2 cup blanched almonds
1/2 cup chopped citron
1 1/2 teaspoons lemon extract

Dissolve yeast and 1 tablespoon sugar in warm water. Cover and allow to bubble up. Cream shortening and sugar in large bowl. Sift together flour, salt, and nutmeg.

Add eggs and scalded milk alternately with flour to the creamed mixture. Stir in yeast mixture. Add fruits and flavoring. Knead until smooth. Cover and let dough rise to double its bulk.

Knead dough again. Shape into ropes about 1 1/2 inches in diameter. For each large stollen make one rope 3 feet long and two that are 2 1/2 feet long. Braid the ropes together, shaping the braid to a point at either end.

Place the braid on a greased cookie sheet. Bake at 400° for 25 minutes or until golden.

2 large stollen

Epiphany Bread

We shall not cease from exploration
And the end of all our exploring
Will be to arrive where we started
And know the place for the first time.

—*T. S. Eliot*

4 cups milk
3 1/2 cups sugar
3 1/2 teaspoons salt
11 eggs
1 cup butter, melted
7 packages yeast (dissolved in 1 1/3 cup warm water)
2 1/2 pounds raisins (soak in 1/4 to 1/2 cup warm water)
16–17 cups flour

In a large heavy pan scald 4 cups milk. Add sugar and salt. Cool. Beat eggs and add with melted butter and dissolved yeast to the cooled milk mixture. Add raisins including the extra water.

Measure 14 cups flour into a large bowl and beat in the above mixture. Add additional flour, but the batter should be a little sticky.

Cover and let rise to double in size and then punch down. Form into loaves and place in greased loaf pans. Let rise in pans until double in size. Bake at 325° for about 50 minutes.

5 loaves, (cake like)

Whole Wheat Buttermilk Bread
(a quick bread from South Africa)

Friendship is a basket of bread from which to eat for years to come. Good loaves fragrant and warm miraculously multiplied; the basket never empty and the bread never stale.

—*Catherine de Vinck*

1 cup white flour
2 heaped cups coarsely ground wholewheat flour
3 tablespoons sesame seed
2 tablespoons toasted wheat germ
1 tablespoon brown sugar or honey
1 teaspoon salt
1 heaped teaspoon of baking soda
2 cups buttermilk

Preheat oven to 400°.

Mix all the dry ingredients together thoroughly. Make a well in the center and add all of the buttermilk at once. Combine ingredients and add a little water if the mixture is too dry.

Grease and flour a bread pan. Pour the mixture into the pan and bake at 400° for about 40 minutes. Cool and serve.

1 loaf

SPRING

Spring bursts today,
For Christ has risen and all the world's at play.

—*Christina Rossetti*

Soups
Minestrone Monastico

At appointed times monks ought to be occupied with holy reading. Each monk shall receive a book from the library, which he should read from cover to cover. These books should be handed out at the beginning of Lent.

—from the Holy Rule of St. Benedict

3 quarts water
4 carrots
1 cup dry white beans
4 potatoes
1 cup green beans, cut in pieces
2 celery stalks
3 onions
  olive oil
1 cup white wine
1 cup macaroni
  tarragon, minced
  salt and pepper to taste
  grated Parmesan cheese

Wash the vegetables and peel the carrots, potatoes, and onions. Cut them in small pieces. Pour the water in a large soup kettle and add all of the vegetables, except the onions. Cook slowly over medium heat for 1 hour.

Sauté the onions in a few tablespoons oil in a large frying pan until golden. Reserve.

After an hour of slow cooking, add the onions, the wine, olive oil to taste (up to 1 cup or more), the macaroni, the tarragon, and the salt and pepper. Continue cooking for another 15 minutes. Cover the pan and allow to simmer for 10 minutes. Serve the minestrone hot, with grated Parmesan cheese.

6–8 servings

Cream of Asparagus Soup

Even if monks live in the desert, far from the tumult of the city and public affairs, they neglect nothing either in their actions or in their words, to make of their heart an inviolable sanctuary and to preserve intact that purity which permits them to enter into communication with God to the degree compatible with human strength.

—*St. John Chrysostom*

1/2 **pound fresh asparagus, cut in 1 inch pieces**
1 **potato, diced**
1 **onion, diced**
1 **medium carrot, sliced**
2 **quarts water**
1 **cup heavy cream**
2 **tablespoons butter**
  salt and pepper to taste

Cook the vegetables in the salted water until they are tender. Pass the soup through a sieve, food mill, or a blender.

Return the soup to the saucepan, add heavy cream, and butter, salt and pepper to taste. Stir and bring almost to a boil. Stir again, cover the pan and simmer for 10 minutes before serving hot.

NOTE: For a soup of thicker consistency, substitute 1 cup of white sauce for the heavy cream.

4–6 servings

Vermicelli Soup
(Potage au vermicelli)

This is the value of the Resurrection—that things unvalued now reveal their worth.

—*Lucy Larcom*

2 1/2 **quarts water**
3 **garlic cloves, minced**
1 **onion, minced**
2 **carrots, cut in small cubes**
6 **vegetable bouillon cubes**
3 **ounces vermicelli noodles**
1/2 **cup fresh parsley, minced**
salt to taste

Bring the water to boil in large soup kettle. Add the bouillon and sliced vegetables, except parsley, and cook for about 15 minutes. Add the vermicelli noodles and continue cooking for another 15 minutes over medium heat.

When the vegetables are tender, add the minced parsley and salt. Cover the kettle and simmer for 10 more minutes before serving hot.

NOTE: The flavor of this easy soup is greatly enhanced when homemade bouillon is used. White wine may also be added to the broth.

6 servings

Main Dishes
Scalloped Parsnips

For there is hope of a tree, if it be cut down, that it will sprout again, and that the tender branch thereof will not cease.

—Job 14:7

10 parsnips
 1 onion, thinly sliced
1/3 cup freshly chopped parsley
 2 cups of tomato sauce (preferably homemade)
1/2 cup bread crumbs
1/2 cup grated cheese of your choice
 salt and pepper to taste

Preheat oven to 375°.

Wash and clean the parsnips. Slice them and boil them for 15 minutes. Drain off the liquid and stir in the onion, parsley, and tomato sauce.

Grease a flat baking dish and spread the parsnip-tomato sauce mixture evenly. Salt if you wish. Cover with bread crumbs and the grated cheese. Bake at 375° for 35 to 40 minutes. Serve hot.

6 servings

Saint Mary of Egypt Fava Beans

(Fèves Sainte-Marie l'Egyptienne)

Saint Mary of Egypt is one of those desert saints who has a timeless appeal to all those who seek God by way of the monastic life. Mary was a 5th century harlot from Alexandria who, one day while in a church in Jerusalem after praying before the icon of the Mother of God, was somehow mysteriously touched by the grace of God. After her conversion, she crossed the river Jordan to live an austere life of prayer and penance. Her feast is celebrated on April 2nd.

12 **ounces fava beans**
2 **leeks, sliced**
2 **onions, sliced**
2 **garlic cloves, minced**
   sesame oil
   parsley
   salt

Soak the beans overnight. Rinse and boil them for about 30 minutes in fresh water until they are tender. Drain.

Sauté the leeks, the onions, and garlic in sesame oil in a large skillet, stirring from time to time until the onions begin to turn golden. Add the cooked beans, 1/3 cup water, salt and parsley. Continue cooking for 15 minutes over low to medium heat with the pan covered. Stir occasionally so that the vegetables do not burn on the bottom, and add water if necessary. Turn down the heat and simmer for an additional 10 to 15 minutes. Serve hot.

4–6 servings

Candied Sweet Potatoes with Raisins

If you wish to put in order the inner dwelling-place of your soul, prepare the material necessary so that the heavenly architect can begin his work. In order for the dwelling to be light, so that the light of heaven can come in, there must be windows, which are our five senses. The door of the abode is Christ . . . who guards both the dwelling and its inhabitants.

—*St. Seraphim of Sarov*

4 tablespoons butter
8 sweet potatoes
1 cup raisins
1 cup brown sugar
1 cup sweet wine
1 cup water
1/2 teaspoon salt

Preheat oven to 300°.

Peel the potatoes and cut them lengthwise in 1/2 inch thick slices.

Melt the butter in a large skillet. Add the potatoes, raisins, and sugar. Stir for 1 or 2 minutes until the potatoes are evenly coated.

Butter a flat baking dish and arrange the potatoes attractively in it. Mix together all the remaining ingredients. Cover the dish and bake at 300° for about 45 minutes. Uncover and continue baking for another 20 minutes. Serve hot.

6–8 servings

Crêpes with Camembert Cheese

(Crêpes au Camembert)

Let the oratory be what it is called, a place of prayer, and let nothing else be done there. Let reverence for God be preserved there.

—*from the Holy Rule of St. Benedict*

1 cup flour
2 eggs
1 1/2 cups milk
4 tablespoons vegetable oil
salt to taste
8 ounces Camembert cheese
4 teaspoons finely chopped chives
(optional)

Place the flour in a mixing bowl, and form a hollow in the center. Add the eggs and beat with an electric mixer. Gradually add the milk and beat until the batter is thoroughly smooth and of a thick, light consistency. Beat in the oil and salt.

Slice the cheese into small pieces and crumble. Add to the batter. Mix well.

Oil or butter a 7-inch crêpe pan. For each crêpe, use about 7 tablespoons of the batter (as much as necessary to cover the bottom of the pan) and swirl around. Cook one side briefly until it turns light brown and then, with the help of a spatula, turn and cook the other side. Roll the crêpes and serve them while still warm.

4–6 servings
(12 to 16 crepes)

Acorn Squash Stuffed with Cottage Cheese

But unless humility, simplicity and goodness adorn our lives, and are associated with prayer, the mere formality of prayer will avail us nothing. And this I say, not of prayer only, but of every other outward exercise or labor undertaken with the notion of virtue.

—*St. Macarius*

2 medium acorn squashes
8 ounces cottage cheese
1/3 finely chopped chives
1/3 cup chopped chervil or parsley
  salt to taste

Cut squash in half and hollow out the insides. Fill a large saucepan with water and bring to boil. Place the squash halves cut side down in the water and boil them for about 15 minutes until they are cooked, but still firm.

While the squash is cooking, thoroughly combine the cottage cheese, chives, and chervil or parsley. Drain the squash halves and fill with the cottage cheese and herbs mixture. Serve immediately.

NOTE: An easy and nutritious dish for a light lunch.

4 servings

Asparagus Stuffed Eggs

In a pleasant spring morning all sins are forgiven. Such a day is a truce to vice. While such a sun holds out to burn, the vilest sinner may return. Through our own recovered innocence we discern the innocence of our neighbors.

—*Henry David Thoreau*

8 eggs, hard-boiled
2 tablespoons minced parsley
1 cup asparagus tips, cooked
1 tablespoon French mustard
   mayonnaise
   salt and pepper to taste

Cut the hard-boiled eggs in half lengthwise. Gently remove the yolks and place them in a bowl. Add the cooked asparagus and parsley and thoroughly mash everything together, or process in a blender until smooth.

Add mustard, enough mayonnaise for moisture, salt and pepper, and blend well. Fill the egg white halves with the mixture, and serve with slices of ripe tomato and olives.

4 servings

Linguine with Broccoli and Tofu

I believe that it is the witness of the monk to the eternal, to preach the tenderness of God, and to live it.

—*Mother Maria*

1/2 **pound linguine**
1/2 **pound tofu**
  3 **cups broccoli spears (florets)**
  8 **garlic cloves, minced**
1/2 **cup olive oil**
1/2 **cup grated cheese of your choice**
    salt and pepper to taste

Cook linguine in a large pot of salted water for about 8 to 9 minutes, until the linguine are tender.

Wash, rinse, and cut the tofu in small cubes. Steam the tofu with the broccoli for about 5 to 7 minutes in a small amount of water.

Brown the garlic in the olive oil, stirring continuously for a minute or two.

Drain the linguine, broccoli, and tofu, and place them in a large serving bowl. Add salt and pepper to taste and pour the garlic sauce over. Mix well, sprinkle with grated cheese, and serve while it is steaming hot.

6 servings

Vegetable-Noodle Casserole

This rule in gardening never forget,
To sow dry and set wet.

—Old Proverb

12 ounces broad egg noodles
 2 cups diced eggplant
 2 medium tomatoes, sliced
 1 green pepper, chopped
 1 onion, chopped
 1 tablespoon chopped parsley
   garlic powder
   salt and pepper
 1 cup grated yellow American cheese
   Parmesan cheese

Preheat oven to 350°.

Cook noodles according to package directions and drain.

Sauté vegetables and seasonings gently in oil until softened. Combine noodles, vegetable mixture, and cheese in a buttered casserole dish. Sprinkle top with Parmesan. Bake at 350° for 30 to 45 minutes.

6 servings

Festive Lasagna

The story of Easter is the story of God's wonderful window of divine surprise.

—*Carl Knudsen*

1 pound lasagna noodles
  oil
3/4 pound ricotta or cottage cheese
1 pound mozzarella cheese
  wheat germ

tomato sauce
  1 large onion, chopped
  1 carrot, thinly sliced
  3 garlic cloves, minced
 12 ounces tomato puree
  7 cups canned tomatoes, strained
    bay leaf
1/4 cup basil, minced
  2 pinches oregano
    salt and pepper

Preheat oven to 375°.

To make sauce, gently fry onion, carrot, and garlic in oil. Stir in tomato puree and strained whole tomatoes. Add bay leaf, basil, and oregano. Simmer about 2 hours, stirring to prevent burning, until sauce is of desired thickness. Salt sparingly at the last minute. Add pepper if a spicier sauce is desired.

Cook noodles according to package directions. Oil the bottom of a large baking dish and arrange the ingredients in liberal layers as follows: sauce, noodles, sauce, noodles, ricotta (cottage cheese), noodles, sauce. Top with sliced mozzarella cheese, sauce, and sprinkle surface with wheat germ. Bake at 375° for about 30 minutes.

6–8 servings

French-Style Fish Fillets with Herbs

(Filets aux herbes)

I believe that without the impetus of love, it is not possible to begin or continue any journey of the spirit. But love, too, must know its measure and its limitations.

—*Sister Thekla*

1 pound firm fish fillets
1/2 cup dry white wine or dry
   vermouth
1/2 cup water
   salt, pepper
1 onion, chopped
   parsley, chives, chervil, thyme
2 tablespoons butter

Preheat oven to 350°.

Arrange the fish fillets in an oven-to-table baking dish.

Combine the wine or vermouth, water, seasonings, onions, and herbs and pour over the fish. Dot with butter. Bake 30 minutes, basting from time to time. Serve from the baking dish, spooning the juices over each portion.

6 servings

Cheese Soufflé

But unless humility, simplicity, and goodness adorn our lives, and are associated with prayer, the mere formality of prayer will avail us nothing. And this I say, not of prayer only, but of every other outward exercise or labor undertaken with a notion of virtue.

—*St. Macarius*

1 **cup grated Parmesan or Romano cheese**
3 **tablespoons margarine or butter**
3 **tablespoons white flour or cornstarch**
1 **cup milk**
  salt, pepper, nutmeg to taste
1/2 **pound grated sharp cheddar cheese**
6 **eggs, separated**

Preheat oven to 375°.

Generously butter a 2-quart soufflé dish and coat the bottom and sides with the Parmesan or Romano cheese, using the entire cup.

Prepare cheese sauce: melt margarine or butter, add flour or cornstarch and stir until smooth. Add milk slowly, stirring and cooking over low to medium heat until thickened. Stir in seasonings and cheddar cheese gradually, beating until smooth. (If too thick, add some milk.)

Add beaten egg yolks to cheese sauce. Cool sauce. Beat egg whites until very stiff and fold into cooled cheese-yolk mixture--don't beat.

Pour mixture into soufflé dish. Bake 30 minutes without opening oven until lightly brown. Serve immediately.

NOTE: For a spinach soufflé, add chopped cooked spinach, well-drained, (1 pound fresh or frozen) and 1 chopped onion, sautéed, to cheese-yolk mixture.

4 servings

Salads
Mixed Salad for Spring

Courage is an inner resolution to go forward despite obstacles; cowardice is submissive surrender to circumstances. Courage breeds creative self-affirmation; cowardice produces destructive self-abnegation. Courage faces fear and masters it; cowardice represses fear and is mastered by it.

—*Martin Luther King, Jr.*

1 1/2 cups fresh green peas
1 1/2 cups green beans, cut in 1-inch
     pieces
    1 small onion, minced
    1 large green pepper, sliced
     oil and vinegar dressing
     parsley
     salt, pepper
3–4 tomatoes
    3 eggs, hard-boiled

Cook peas and green beans. Drain and rinse briefly in cold water. Toss still-warm peas and beans with onion, dressing, seasonings, parsley, and green pepper. Chill.

Serve either on a platter surrounded with rings of sliced tomatoes and sliced eggs or stuff salad into hollowed-out tomatoes and surround by egg slices. Good with mayonnaise.

6 servings

Raw Spinach-Mushroom Salad

The yoke of Christ is sweet and his burden light unto refreshment for those who submit to it; but all things alien to the teachings of the Gospel are heavy and burdensome.

—from the Short Rules of St. Basil

1 pound raw spinach, trimmed and
  torn in bite-size pieces
1 pound mushrooms, sliced
1 red apple, peeled and sliced
1 small onion, thinly sliced
2 eggs, hard-boiled and chopped

Dressing
6 tablespoons oil
2 tablespoons vinegar
1/2 teaspoon salt
1/2 teaspoon pepper
  dash of tamari or soy sauce

Mix and toss together the spinach, mushrooms, apple, onion, and chopped eggs.

Prepare a salad dressing by mixing the oil, vinegar, soy sauce, salt, and pepper. Mix well and pour over the salad. Toss lightly and serve.

NOTE: Non-vegetarians can sprinkle crisp bacon bits on salad.

6–8 servings

Rice Salad
(Riz en salade)

God can bring summer out of winter, though we have no spring. All occasions invite his mercies, and all times are his seasons.

—*John Donne*

1 cup rice
1/2 cup pitted green olives, chopped
1/2 cup pitted black olives, chopped
olive oil
lemon juice
salt and pepper
1/3 cup parsley, finely chopped

Place the rice in a saucepan with 1 tablespoon oil, salt and pepper, and stir well. Add 2 cups water, cover tightly and bring the water to a rapid boil. Lower the heat and cook the rice slowly for about 20 minutes until all of the water is absorbed. When the rice is tender, allow it to cool in the refrigerator for at least an hour.

Mix the rice and the olives in a large bowl. Add olive oil, lemon juice, salt and pepper, according to taste, and mix well. Sprinkle the chopped parsley on the top and serve the salad cold.

NOTE: This delightful salad can be served on a large platter with cherry tomatoes and slices of hard-boiled eggs.

4 servings

Mediterranean Lentil Salad

Let all be silent at the table. No whispering or noise is to be heard, only the voice of the reader. The monks shall pass to one another the food and drink as they have need of it, so that no one may ask for anything. If something is missing, then let it be asked for with a signal rather than verbally.

—from the Holy Rule of St. Benedict

2 cups cooked lentils (drained)
1 onion, finely chopped
5 ounces pitted olives, chopped
5 ounces marinated artichokes, chopped
4 ounces chopped pimento

Vinaigrette
2/3 cup olive oil
1/4 cup wine vinegar
1 tablespoon mustard
  salt and pepper to taste

Place all of the salad ingredients in a large bowl and refrigerate for at least 1 hour.

Just before serving, prepare the vinaigrette according to directions in The Basics section, and pour over the salad. Mix well and serve cold.

6 servings

Desserts and Breads
Saint Seraphim's Cake

Saint Seraphim is a Russian saint from the 18th century who was twenty years old when he entered the monastery at Sarov. His life was similar to that of the Desert Fathers of 4th century Egypt. He lived alone in a forest hermitage where he cultivated a small garden, studied Scripture and the writings of the monastic Fathers, and devoted himself to continual prayer. After his health began to fail, he continued his life of seclusion in a small cell in the monastery. A saint of remarkable spiritual insights and prophetic gifts, he was observed in extasis, his facial transfiguration producing a "blinding light."

4 ounces sweet butter or margarine
1 cup sugar
2 eggs
3/4 cup cocoa
1/2 teaspoon salt
2 cups unsifted flour
2 teaspoons baking powder
1/2 teaspoon baking soda
1 cup milk
1 teaspoon vanilla
1/3 cup rum

Preheat oven to 350°.

Cream the butter or margarine and sugar together. Add the eggs one at a time beating thoroughly. Add the cocoa and beat another minute.

Sift the flour, salt, baking powder, and the soda into a deep bowl. Combine the milk, vanilla, and rum. Add the dry ingredients slowly to the chocolate mixture, alternating with the wet ingredients. Blend well until totally smooth.

Grease and flour two 9-inch round cake pans. Divide the cake mixture into them and bake for 35 minutes at 350°. Allow the cake to cool in the pans.

8 servings

Benedictine Rhubarb and Raisin Pudding

The only justification for the monastic life lies simply in the fact that God calls some people to it. For the monk himself there is no problem. He comes to undertake his life of prayer and work and discipline in the community simply because he knows that that is what God wants him to do. He can, therefore, not do anything else.

—Sister Thekla

8 slices whole wheat bread, cubed
1 1/2 cups milk
4 tablespoons butter, melted
4 eggs
1 cup sugar, honey, or molasses, depending on taste
1 cup rhubarb, sliced and cooked
1 cup raisins
pinch of salt, nutmeg and cinnamon

Preheat oven to 350°.

Place the cubed bread in a mixing bowl. Mix the butter and the milk and pour over bread. Let stand for at least 20 minutes.

Beat the eggs in a deep bowl; add the remaining ingredients and mix well. Combine the egg mixture with the bread and milk mixture.

Butter a flat baking dish and pour the mixture into it. Bake at 350° for about 45 minutes. Serve warm or cold.

8 servings

Monastery Whole Wheat Bread

The bread which you do not use is the bread of the hungry; the garment hanging in your wardrobe is the garment of the one who is naked; the shoes you do not wear are the shoes of the one who is barefoot; the money that you keep locked away is the money of the poor; the acts of charity that you do not perform are so many injustices that you commit.

—*St. Basil the Great*

3/4 cup honey
1/4 cup molasses
  3 cups boiling water
  1 cup cold water
  3 packages dry yeast
1/4 vegetable oil
10 cups whole wheat flour
  1 teaspoon salt

Preheat oven to 350°.

Place honey and molasses in large bowl. Stir in hot water, then add cold water. When liquid is lukewarm, sprinkle yeast evenly over mixture to activate yeast. Add oil and gradually stir in flour and salt.

Knead on well-floured bread board until mixture is even. Place in greased bowl and cover with damp towel. Set in warm place to rise for 1 hour.

Punch down and knead. Let rise again for 45 minutes. Knead. Shape and place in well-greased loaf pans. Let rise for 30 minutes. Bake at 350° for about 30 minutes.

3 loaves

Easter Bread

May Easter Day
To thy heart say,
   "Christ died and rose for thee."
May Easter night
On thy heart write,
   "O Christ, I live for thee."

—*Anonymous*

2 cups milk, scalded
1 package yeast
6 cups flour
5 tablespoons shortening
1 cup sugar
2 eggs, well beaten
1 1/2 teaspoon salt
1/2 cup raisins
1/2 cup candied peel
1 teaspoon nutmeg
1 egg, slightly beaten

Cool milk to lukewarm and dissolve yeast in it. Add 2 cups flour and beat well.

Cream shortening with sugar; add eggs and beat well. Add milk mixture with salt and remaining flour. Knead well; let rise in a warm place for about 1 1/2 hours. Work in remaining ingredients except for egg, and knead on floured board until dough does not stick.

Place in a greased bowl, rub with butter, cover, and let rise until double in bulk. Knead again, and shape into 2 rings on a cookie sheet. Brush lightly with the beaten egg, and let rise until double again. Bake at 400° for 15 minutes, then reduce heat to 350° and bake for 15 minutes more.

2 ring-shaped loaves

Paschal Spice Ring

For I remember it is Easter morn,
And life and love and peace are all new born.

—*Alice Palmer*

3 tablespoons shortening
1 cup sugar
1 teaspoon baking soda
10 3/4 ounces condensed tomato soup
2 cups flour
1 teaspoon cinnamon
1 teaspoon each mace, nutmeg, and cloves, mixed
1 1/2 cups raisins or candied fruit peel

orange icing
4 tablespoons soft margarine or butter
1/4 teaspoon salt
1/2 pound confectioners' sugar
1/4 cup frozen orange juice concentrate, thawed

Preheat oven to 325°.

Cream shortening and sugar. Stir soda into soup. Sift flour and spices together and combine with the creamed shortening and sugar. Stir well. Add the soup and raisins or candied fruit peel. Mix well. Bake in a 10-inch tube pan at 325° for 35 minutes. Remove from pan and allow to cool.

To make icing: cream butter or margarine, add salt, a little sugar and work together well. Add additional sugar and orange juice concentrate alternately in small portions, mixing thoroughly until icing is of good spreading consistency. Frost cake and when icing has set, place a candle in the hole in the center. Dripping melted wax at the base will help it stand securely.

Pentecost Cream

Prayer, fasting and all other Christian undertakings are good in themselves; however, the performing of these things is not the end of our life because they are only the means. The true goal of the Christian life is to acquire the Holy Spirit.

—*St. Seraphim of Sarov*

4 eggs
1/2 to 3/4 cup sugar
1/2 cup butter
1 quart milk
1/2 cup flour
  peel of 1/2 lemon, sliced in thin strips
1/2 teaspoon anise
1/4 teaspoon nutmeg
1 teaspoon vanilla
1 package (10 to 12) anisette spongecake fingers
2 cups sliced peaches
1/2 pint whipping cream
1/2 teaspoon brandy
1/2 cup confectioners' sugar
  small pinch nutmeg

Cream together eggs and sugar.

In a saucepan, melt butter; blend flour with 1 cup of milk and add it with rest of milk and lemon peel to saucepan. Cook, stirring until it starts to thicken, but do not boil. Stir in the sugar-egg mixture, spices and vanilla. When thickened, remove lemon peel.

In a flat baking dish, arrange alternate layers of this mixture with cake fingers and sliced peaches. End with a cream layer on top.

Whip cream; add brandy, confectioners' sugar, and nutmeg. Spread on top of cake layer. Chill 4–8 hours.

8 servings

Whitsun Cake

Why did Christ refer to the grace of the Spirit under the name of water? Because through water all vegetables and animals live. Because the water of rain comes down from heaven, and though rain comes down in one form, its effects take many forms. Yea, one spring watered all of paradise, and the same rain falls on the whole world, yet it becomes white in the lily, red in the rose, purple in the violet.

—*St. Cyril of Jerusalem*

2/3 cup milk
1 cup sugar
1 1/3 cups sifted flour
3 teaspoons baking powder
2 egg whites
1/4 teaspoon cream of tartar
1/4 teaspoon salt
1 teaspoon vanilla
15 large strawberries
1 1/2 cups confectioners' sugar
2 tablespoons butter or margarine

Preheat oven to 350°.

Scald milk and allow to cool. Sift sugar, flour, and baking powder together 3 times. Add cooled milk gradually, beating constantly.

Beat egg whites with cream of tartar, salt, and vanilla, for 1 1/2 to 2 minutes, or until the egg whites refuse to slip when the bowl is tipped. Fold into flour mixture.

Bake in an ungreased 7-inch tube pan at 350° for 45 minutes or until the cake is golden brown and firm to the touch. Invert the cake on a rack until cool.

Hull and clean 15 large strawberries. Crush 8 with a fork, and sweeten to taste. Cream the butter or margarine and confectioners' sugar in a bowl, add enough crushed berries and juice to make a mixture of spreading consistency. Frost the cake and top with 7 whole strawberries as a reminder of the gifts of the Holy Spirit.

SUMMER

As down in the sunless retreats of the ocean,
Sweet flowers are springing no mortal can see,
So, deep in my soul the still prayer of devotion
Unheard by the world rises silent to Thee.

—*Thomas Moore*

Soups and Appetizers
Parsley Soup
(Potage au persil)

They said of Abba Macarius the Great that he became, as it is written, a god upon earth because just as God protects the world, so Abba Macarius would cover the faults that he saw as though he did not see them, and those which he heard as though he did not hear them.

—from the Sayings of the Desert Fathers

3 medium tomatoes
4 tablespoons olive oil
1 leek, finely chopped
1 onion, chopped and minced
3 garlic cloves, minced
1 big bunch parsley, finely chopped
1 cup dry white wine
   salt and pepper to taste

Boil the tomatoes for 5 minutes, cool them in cold water, and then peel. Slice lengthwise and discard the pulp and seeds.

Pour the olive oil into a soup kettle, add the leek and the onion and sauté until they begin to brown. Add the tomatoes, garlic, wine, 4 1/2 cups water, salt and pepper. Boil over low to medium heat for 20 minutes. Add the parsley and continue cooking the soup for another 10 minutes. Process soup in a blender. Serve hot or refrigerate for a few hours and serve cold.

4 servings

Quick Vichyssoise

All guests who arrive to the monastery should be welcomed as Christ, because he will say, "I was a stranger and you took me in." Show them every courtesy, especially to servants of God and pilgrims.

—from the Holy Rule of St. Benedict

4 tablespoons butter or margarine
4 leeks, finely sliced
4 potatoes, diced
3 bouillon cubes (or use vegetable stock in place of water)
1 bouquet garni (1 bay leaf, 1 sprig of thyme and parsley tied together)
2 cups milk
1 cup heavy cream
  salt and fresh pepper to taste
  fresh parsley or mint leaves for optional garnish

Melt the butter or margarine in a large soup kettle. Add the leeks and cook over low heat for 5 to 6 minutes, or until tender. Add the potatoes, bouillon, bouquet garni, milk, salt and pepper, and 2 cups of water (more if desired.)

Raise the heat to medium and allow the soup to cook slowly for 25 to 30 minutes. Turn down the heat and simmer the soup for an additional 10 minutes. Remove the bouquet garni and mix the soup in a blender. Chill the soup for a few hours and just before serving, add the heavy cream and stir thoroughly. Garnish the cold soup with finely chopped parsley or mint leaves, if you wish.

4–6 servings

Saint Macarius Cucumbers
(Concombres Saint Macaire)

Saint Macarius the Elder was a desert monk who lived in Egypt from the year 300 to 390 A.D. Following the example of St. Anthony the Great, he withdrew into the wilderness when he was thirty years old and stayed there another six decades. He was renowned for his silent and austere life and for his wisdom. Because he was one of the first monks to retire to the desert, he is rightly considered to be one of the fathers of early monasticism.

2 cucumbers
6 tablespoons heavy cream
1 lemon
  chervil and coriander, finely chopped
  salt

Peel the cucumbers and cut in thin slices. Stand in cold salted water for 3 hours. Rinse the cucumbers in cold water and drain thoroughly.

Mix well the heavy cream and juice from 1 lemon with the chervil and coriander. Pour over the cucumbers and toss gently. Serve cold.

2 servings

Bread Pissaladière

We are going to establish a school for God's service. In founding it we hope to introduce nothing harsh or burdensome. For preserving charity or correcting faults, it may be necessary at times, by reason of justice, to be slightly more severe. Do not fear this and retreat, for the path to salvation is long and the entrance is narrow.

—from the Holy Rule of St. Benedict

1 cup olive oil
1 onion, sliced
15 ounces pitted black olives
4 tablespoons herbs provencales
   (basil, thyme, rosemary)
4 ripe tomatoes, sliced
1 loaf French bread, sliced
   garlic cloves and anchovies
   (optional)

Preheat oven to 400°.

Pour the olive oil into a blender; add the onion, black olives, and herbs (garlic and anchovies, if desired) and blend thoroughly until smooth.

Cover the slices of bread with the spread (about 4 slices per person), and place on a greased or oiled baking sheet.

Arrange the tomatoes on top. If you wish, sprinkle some herbs or grated cheese on the tomatoes. Place in the oven at 400° for 15 minutes or under the broiler for a few minutes until the tomatoes are cooked. Serve as appetizers or canapes before dinner. This is especially good in mid-summer when tomatoes are in season.

4 servings

Main Dishes

Tuna Mousse

A Brother asked Abba Poemen, "Is it better to speak or be silent?" The old man said to him, "One who speaks for God's sake does well; but one who is silent for God's sake also does well."

—*from the Sayings of the Desert Fathers*

1 envelope unflavored gelatin
2 tablespoons lemon juice
1/2 cup boiling chicken broth or an all-vegetable broth
1/2 cup mayonnaise
1/4 cup milk
2 tablespoons chopped parsley
1 tablespoon finely chopped parsley
1 teaspoon dried dill (fresh dill is better)
1 teaspoon Dijon mustard
1/4 teaspoon white pepper
7 ounces tuna, drained and flaked
1 cup shredded cucumber

In a deep mixing bowl, soften the gelatin in the lemon juice. Add the boiling broth and stir to dissolve the gelatin.

Add the remaining ingredients, except the tuna and the cucumber, and mix everything well. Chill for about 30 minutes until slightly thickened. Fold in the tuna and cucumber and beat until mixture turns frothy.

Pour the mixture into a serving bowl or mold and chill until firm. Serve cold.

4 servings

Cauliflower Santa Lucia

They cannot be deemed worthy of the kingdom of heaven who do not imitate in their relations with one another the equality which is observed by children among themselves.

—from the Short Rules of St. Basil

1 head cauliflower
3 tablespoons butter
2 carrots, diced
1 onion, finely chopped
1 cup white vermouth or white wine
salt and pepper to taste
dash dried mustard
finely grated cheese of your choice

Preheat oven to 350°.

Separate the cauliflower florets. Slice the stems in 1-inch pieces. Melt the butter into a large skillet; add the cauliflower, carrots and onion. Sauté the vegetables for about 3 minutes. Add the vermouth or wine, salt and pepper, mustard, and continue cooking over medium heat for another 3 minutes.

Butter a baking dish that has a lid. Place the vegetables and the sauce in it. Cover the dish and bake at 350° for 20 minutes. Sprinkle on the finely grated cheese and continue baking for another 10 minutes. Serve hot.

4 servings

Potato and Carrot Puff

O light that never fades, as the light of day now streams through these windows and floods this room, so let me open to You the windows of my heart, that all my life may be filled by the radiance of Your presence. . . . Let there be nothing within me to darken the brightness of the day.

—John Baillie

8 large potatoes
6 large carrots
6 tablespoons butter
4 egg yolks
1 cup milk
4 egg whites
  salt and pepper to taste

Preheat oven to 350°.

Wash and peel the potatoes and carrots. Boil until done, then drain and mash together thoroughly.

Beat the eggs yolks and milk in a deep bowl. Add the mashed potatoes and carrots, salt and pepper, and mix well.

Beat the egg whites until stiff. Fold the beaten whites into the potato-carrot mixture. Grease a baking dish well and pour the mixture into it. Bake at 350° for 20 to 25 minutes until the top turns golden brown. Serve hot.

6 servings

Avocado Omelette
(Omelette à l'avocat)

He prayeth best who loveth best
All things both great and small;
For the dear God who loveth us,
He made and loveth all.

—*Samuel Taylor Coleridge in*
"The Rime of the Ancient Mariner"

5 eggs
  salt and pepper to taste
  pinch of chervil, finely chopped
1 firm avocado
  olive oil

Break the eggs into a bowl and beat vigorously. Add salt and pepper and chervil, and beat some more.

Peel the avocado and dice in cubes. Pour sufficient oil into an omelette pan and heat. When the oil is hot, place the avocado in the pan, stir, and cook for a few seconds. Pour the egg mixture on top and cook, lifting the edges with a spatula to permit the uncooked egg to run under. When one side of the omelette is done, carefully fold in half. (Do not overcook, since the omelette should remain moist inside.) Slide the omelette onto a previously warmed plate and serve immediately.

2 servings

Egg Noodles with Basil and Cheese

In the deserts of the heart
Let the healing fountain start;
In the prison of his days
Teach the free man how to praise.

—*W. H. Auden*

1 pound egg noodles
4 tablespoons butter
4 tablespoons olive oil
1 cup thinly chopped fresh basil
4 garlic cloves, finely chopped
3/4 cup grated Romano or Parmesan
    cheese
    salt and freshly ground pepper to
    taste

In a large pot bring 4 quarts of salted water to boil. Add the noodles. Cook for about 10 minutes, stirring from time to time, then drain.

Sauté the basil and garlic in the butter and olive oil for a minute or two. Combine all the ingredients in a casserole, and serve hot with additional cheese on the side for those who wish to add more.

NOTE: This simple and appetizing recipe can be adapted to any kind of pasta or noodles.

6 servings

Vegetable-Cheese Casserole

Pride is to stick to one's own judgment, without taking into account God's transforming creative love.

—*Mother Maria*

2 medium eggplants (or 1 large)
3 cups milk
6 eggs, well beaten
2 teaspoons cornstarch
1 small onion, chopped
8 ounces chopped frozen spinach, thawed and drained
· salt, pepper, dash of nutmeg
· bread slices seasoned with garlic salt and oregano
· coarsely grated cheddar cheese

Preheat oven to 350°.

Slice and parboil eggplants. Combine all other ingredients except bread and cheese.

Butter a large casserole dish. Fill with alternating layers: milk mixture (on bottom), bread slices, milk mixture, cheese, eggplant slices, milk mixture. Repeat layers ending with milk mixture and cheese on top. Bake at 350° until heated through, about 1 hour.

8 servings

Spinach Casserole with Tomato Topping

Be merry, really merry. The life of the true Christian should be a perpetual jubilee—a prelude to the festivals of eternity.

—*St. Theophane Vernard*

white sauce

6 tablespoons butter
6 tablespoons flour
3 cups milk
1 1/2 teaspoons salt
1/8 teaspoon pepper
dash nutmeg

4 eggs, beaten
1 1/2 to 2 cups cubed stale whole wheat bread
16 ounces frozen chopped spinach, thawed and drained or equivalent fresh spinach
sliced cheddar cheese

topping

2–3 fresh tomatoes
1 large onion, chopped
oregano, parsley, salt, pepper

Preheat oven to 350°.

Make white sauce according to instructions in The Basics section. Season with nutmeg. Add beaten eggs, cubed bread, and spinach, and mix thoroughly.

Place the mixture in a buttered casserole dish. Cover with sliced cheese.

Cut tomatoes into thick slices and fry briefly with chopped onion, oregano, parsley, salt, and pepper. Place tomato slices and seasonings on top of casserole. Bake at 350° until bubbly and browned, about 1 hour.

6 servings

Creamed Mushrooms on Toast

(Farce aux champignons)

The flow of prayer is like the Gulf Stream, imparting warmth to all that is cold, melting all that is hard to life.

—*Abraham Joshua Heschel*

1/2 **pound mushrooms, washed and sliced**
2 **tablespoons butter**
1 **tablespoon oil**
1/4 **cup diced onion or shallot**
   salt, pepper (garlic salt, optional)

white sauce
4 **tablespoons butter**
4 **tablespoons flour**
2 **cups milk**

6 **slices toast**

Sauté mushrooms in 2 tablespoons butter and 1 tablespoon oil until they begin to brown; add onion, salt, pepper (and optional garlic salt) and continue sautéeing gently until onion is transparent.

Make a white sauce according to instructions in The Basics section. Season to taste. Stir mushrooms and onions into sauce.

Serve sauce over slices of toast. You may wish to place sauce covered toast under a broiler for a few minutes until sauce is bubbly and slightly brown on top.

6 servings

Tivoli Corn Scallop

The past must be abandoned to God's mercy, the present to our fidelity, and the future to divine providence.

—St. John Vianney

2 eggs
17 ounces cream style corn
1/2 cup crushed soda crackers
1/4 cup undiluted evaporated milk
1/4 cup chopped green pepper
1 teaspoon chopped onion
1/2 teaspoon sugar
1/4 cup butter or margarine, melted
1/4 cup finely shredded carrot
1 tablespoon chopped celery
6 drops Tabasco
1/2 teaspoon salt
1/2 cup shredded cheddar cheese
paprika

Preheat oven to 350°.

In large bowl, beat eggs with fork. Add the remaining ingredients, except cheese and paprika, and mix thoroughly. Put in a greased 8-inch square baking dish. Sprinkle with cheese and paprika. Bake at 350° for 30 minutes or until mixture is set and top is golden brown. (A sprinkling of sesame seeds, about 1/4 cup, gives a nice crunch.)

6–8 servings

Cloister Carrots

It may be objected that the monastic movement attempted to cure economic evils by running away from them, and that the monk's cell provided a last refuge for those who "had despaired of the state." This is very far from the case. The monastic movement . . . made an honest endeavor to correct in the world at large the results of an economic system which it could not alter.

—*E. F. Morison, Oxford*

10 large carrots
1 quart milk
1 cup raisins
1/2 cup blanched, slivered almonds
2 tablespoons brown sugar

Wash and peel the carrots; cut in very thin slices.

Combine the carrots, raisins, almonds, and the brown sugar with 1 quart of milk in a pot.

Bring to boil and then simmer for 1 hour, stirring occasionally. Serve hot in the winter or chill and serve cold in the summer.

6–8 servings

Sautéed Zucchini

Do not in spirit become discontented, for discontent lodges in the bosom of a fool. Do not say: How is it that former times were better than these? For it is not in wisdom that you ask this. . . . On a good day enjoy the good things, and on an evil day consider: both the one and the other God has made.

—Ecclesiates 7:9-10, 14

4 medium zucchinis
1/2 cup oil or butter
2 tablespoons chopped scallions or
   shallots
2 tablespoons chopped parsley
   salt and fresh pepper

Wash zucchinis and cut into sticks without peeling or removing the seeds. Boil in salted water for 2 minutes. Drain.

Just before serving, pour the oil (olive oil is best) or melt the butter in a pan and add the zucchini immediately. Add chopped scallions and parsley, and salt and pepper according to taste. Sauté 5 minutes and serve when warm and tender.

4–6 servings

Toledo Spanish Tuna

Meditation with great mental industry plods along the steep and laborious road, keeping the end in view. Contemplation on a free wing circles around with great nimbleness wherever the impulse takes it. Meditation investigates; contemplation wonders.

—*Richard of St. Victor*

1/4 cup oil
1 cup rice
1 medium onion, sliced thin
1/3 cup chopped green pepper
1 garlic clove, minced
20 ounces canned tomatoes
1/2 cup tomato juice
1 1/2 cups water
8 ounces sliced or canned mushrooms
1 teaspoon salt
dash of cayenne
7 ounces chunk-style tuna, drained and flaked

Heat oil in saucepan or large skillet. Add rice. Sauté until golden. Add onions, green pepper, garlic clove, tomatoes, tomato juice, water, mushrooms, salt and cayenne.

Cook, covered, over low heat for 35 to 40 minutes or until rice is done, stirring occasionally. Add tuna. Cover and heat through. Serve hot.

4 servings

Scalloped Fish Sainte-Melanie

Don't think of God as a very stern judge and punisher. He is very merciful. . . . We must not despair, for there is no sin that exceeds God's compassion. It is always the devil that brings despair; one must not listen to him.

—letter from a Russian monk

1 1/2 pounds fish fillets
10 3/4 ounces condensed mushroom
     soup
  2 tablespoons diced green pepper
  1 can green peas (drained)
1/4 cup lemon juice
     salt, pepper to taste
     dash Worcestershire sauce
  4 slices bread, lightly toasted and
     cubed
1/4 cup melted butter
     grated cheese of your choice
     (optional)

Preheat oven to 350°.

Cut fish fillets into 1/2-inch cubes. Combine with all other ingredients, except bread crumbs and butter, and place in well-greased baking dish.

Cover with bread cubes which have been mixed with melted butter, or sprinkle with grated cheese. Bake at 350° until heated through and brown on top (about 1 hour).

4 servings

Spinach Crêpes

A good name is better than ointment, and the day of death than the day of birth. . . . Better is the end of speech than its beginning; better is the patient spirit than the lofty spirit.

—*Ecclesiastes 7:1,8*

2 eggs
1 cup flour
1 cup milk

filling
   3 tablespoons butter
   1 chopped onion
   2 garlic cloves, minced
   1 bunch fresh spinach, washed and dried and chopped, or 8 ounces frozen, thawed, drained and chopped
   4 eggs, hard-boiled and chopped
   1 cup coarsely grated cheddar cheese

cream sauce
   3 tablespoons butter
   3 tablespoons flour
1 1/2 cups milk
   dash nutmeg
   salt and pepper

Preheat oven to 300°.

Make crêpe batter by beating the 2 eggs thoroughly. Then beat in the flour. Stir in 1 cup milk. Put the batter in the refrigerator to rest while you prepare the filling.

In a nonaluminum pan (aluminum tends to blacken spinach and/or make it taste bitter and acidy), melt butter. Gently sauté (don't brown) the onion, then add garlic and chopped spinach. If fresh spinach is used, cover for about 2 minutes to wilt it down. Turn off heat. Add chopped eggs and cheese.

Make thin crêpes, according to directions on page 46. Make cream sauce following method in The Basics section. Place a spoonful of the filling on each crêpe, roll up and arrange in baking dish. Cover with cream sauce. Bake at 300° for 15 minutes.

4–6 servings

Salads
Greens and Beets Salad

I God am in your midst.
Whoever knows me can never fall.
Not in the height, nor in the depth, nor in the breadth.
For I am love, that the vast expanses of evil can never still.

—*St. Hildegard of Bingen*

1 1/2 pounds medium beets
   1 head romaine lettuce
1/2 cup olive oil
   2 tablespoons cider vinegar
1/2 teaspoon salt
1/2 teaspoon freshly ground pepper
   2 tablespoons chopped scallions
   1 tablespoon Dijon mustard

Cut the tops off the beets and put the beets in a pan with boiling water. Cook for 30 minutes or until tender. Drain and cool, then peel, and cut into thin slices.

Tear the romaine into bit-size pieces and mix with the beet slices. Combine the oil, vinegar, salt, pepper, scallions, and mustard. Mix well and pour over the beets and romaine. Serve.

6 servings

Italian Corn Salad
(Salade de maïs Italienne)

Oh how an ignorant and simple soul, who knows only how to love God without loving self, surpasses all the learned! The Spirit intimates all truth to it without detailed study; for by an intimate, profound enlightenment, an enlightenment of truth, experience, and feeling, it makes it realize that it itself is nothing and that God is everything.

—*J. B. Bossuet*

1 green pepper, thinly sliced
1 red pepper, thinly sliced
2 red onions, thinly sliced
12 ounces canned corn
3 tablespoons minced parsley

vinaigrette
6 tablespoons olive oil
3 tablespoons wine vinegar
salt and pepper to taste

Wash and slice the peppers and onions. Place them in a large salad bowl. Drain the corn thoroughly and mix with the onions and peppers.

Prepare a simple vinaigrette by mixing the olive oil, vinegar, salt and pepper. Pour the vinaigrette over the salad and mix well. Refrigerate for 30 minutes. Sprinkle the parsley on the top of the salad before serving.

4 servings

Fennel Salad
(Fenouil en salade)

Better is a dish of herbs where love is than a fatted ox and hatred with it.

—Proverbs 15:17

4 fresh fennel bulbs
1 red onion, thinly sliced
4 ripe medium tomatoes

dressing
1/2 cup olive oil
   juice of one lemon
6 tablespoons tarragon vinegar
3 tablespoons fresh coriander, finely
   chopped, or parsley
   salt and fresh pepper to taste

Trim off and discard the stems and outer skin of the fennels. Cook them in boiling water for exactly 30 minutes. Rinse them in cold water and allow them to cool. Cut into quarters.

Place the quartered fennels into a salad bowl. Add the thinly sliced onion and the tomatoes cut in quarters. Combine the dressing ingredients according to directions in The Basics section. Pour over the salad and toss before serving.

NOTE: Crumbled hard-boiled eggs are an attractive garnish for this salad.

4 servings

Fresh Mushroom and Watercress Salad

It is written: "An altar of earth thou shalt make unto Me . . . and if thou make Me an altar of stone, thou shalt not build it of hewn stones, for if thou lift up thy tool upon it, thou hast profaned it." The altar of earth is the altar of silence, which pleases God beyond all else. But if you do not make an altar of words, do not hew and chisel them, for such artifice would profane it.

—Hasidic saying

1 tablespoon Dijon mustard
(French, preferably)
1/4 cup olive oil
2 tablespoons apple cider vinegar
3 tablespoons chopped scallions
salt and pepper to taste
1/2 pound fresh mushrooms
1 bunch watercress
1 head romaine lettuce

Place mustard and olive oil in a bowl and mix thoroughly with a wire whisk. Add the vinegar, scallions, salt, and pepper and whisk again. Clean the mushrooms, slice thinly and mix with the dressing. Chill until ready to use.

Wash and drain well both the watercress and romaine lettuce. Break into bite-size pieces. When ready to serve the salad, pour the dressing over and mix well.

8 servings

Desserts

Tutti-Frutti Salad

We should not be eager to have the necessities of life in abundance, nor seek after luxury or satiety; but we should be free from every form of avarice and ostentation.

—from the Short Rules of St. Basil

1 ripe melon, diced
2 pears, sliced
2 apples, sliced
1 orange, diced
1 banana, sliced (optional)
1/2 cup seedless raisins
1/3 cup brown sugar
4 teaspoons lemon juice
1/2 cup Porto wine or another sweet
    wine

Mix all of the fruits in a large salad bowl with the sugar and lemon juice. Refrigerate for at least 1 hour.

Just before serving, pour the Porto wine over the fruit and mix thoroughly. Serve cold.

8 servings

Millbrook Prune Pudding

W e should not be vacillating but steadfast in the faith and staunch in cleaving to the good things which are in the Lord.

—from the Short Rules of St. Basil

1/2   **pound prunes**
1 3/4   **cups stale bread crumbs**
1/3   **cup brown sugar**
4   **tablespoons butter**
1/4   **cup cognac**
2   **tablespoons lemon juice**
1/2   **cup prune juice**

Preheat oven to 375°.

Cook the prunes until they are tender. Cool, pit, and slice them in halves. Grease a square baking dish well and carefully arrange layers of stale bread crumbs (use 3/4 cup per layer), sliced prunes, sugar, and small dots of butter. Repeat. Cover the top with remaining 1/4 cup dried crumbs and what is left of the butter.

Pour cognac, lemon juice, and prune juice into a container. Shake and mix thoroughly. Pour this liquid over the pudding mixture. Bake at 375° for 35 to 40 minutes. Allow to cool before serving.

4–6 servings

Melon with Strawberries and Anisette

(Melon à l'anisette et aux fraises)

If there is righteousness in the heart, there will be beauty in the character. If there is beauty in the character, there will be harmony in the home. If there is harmony in the home, there will be order in the nation. When there is order in the nation, there will be peace on earth.

—*Sathya Sai Baba*

2 cantaloupe melons
1/2 cup sugar
4 tablespoons anisette
32 fresh strawberries

Peel the melons and remove seeds. Cut in small slices and mash into a purée. Add the sugar and the anisette and mix everything thoroughly. Refrigerate for at least 2 hours.

Spoon the purée into chilled glass dishes and arrange whole strawberries on the top.

NOTE: This is a quick and easy dessert to prepare on a hot summer day.

4 servings

Peach and Banana Sorbet

There is but one point in the universe where God communicates with us, and that is the center of our own soul.

—*Archbishop Ullathorne*

4 cups sugar
2 teaspoons vanilla
4 cups sliced peaches
2 ripe bananas
  juice of 4 lemons
  juice of 4 oranges
2 tablespoons peach liqueur

Stir and dissolve the sugar in 4 cups of water over low to medium heat. Stir in the vanilla and remove from heat and cool completely.

Purée the peaches and bananas in a blender or food processor. Add the lemon and orange juices and liqueur to the cooled syrup and combine with the fruit purée in the processor or blender. Process only to mix well. (Work in two batches, if necessary.) Divide the sorbet into 6 or 8 individual molds or serving dishes and freeze until ready to be served.

NOTE: This dessert is easy to prepare and especially pleasant during the hot summer months.

6–8 servings

Peach or Pear Compote

Oh, how happy are the alleluias of heaven! Here below we sing it in anxiety and pain; up there we will sing it in peace!

—*St. Augustine*

2 pounds peaches
3/4 cup water
1 1/4 cups sugar

Peel peaches, remove pits, and cut in half. Heat water and sugar together. When sugar is completely dissolved, add peaches. Simmer over low heat for about 15 minutes. To enhance taste, add 1 tablespoon white wine, or your favorite liqueur.

6 servings

2 pounds pears
1 cup sugar (or more)
3/4 cup water
1 1/4 cup wine (white, preferably)
1 tablespoon rum

If the pears are small, peel and leave whole. If they are larger, peel and cut in halves or quarters and remove seeds. Bring the sugar and liquid to a boil, stirring constantly. Remove from the heat as soon as it begins to boil. Add the pears. Cook gently for about 20 minutes. Refrigerate for at least 1 hour. Just before serving, add 1 tablespoon rum to the compote.

6 servings

Barrytown Apple Crumble

For we shall see verily in heaven, without end, that we shall have grievously sinned in this life, and notwithstanding this, we shall see that we were never hurt in God's love, nor were of less price in God's sight. For hard and marvelous is that love which may not, nor will not, be broken for trespass.

—Julian of Norwich

4–6 apples, sliced
1 cup flour
1/2 cup sugar
1 teaspoon baking powder
1/4 teaspoon salt
1 egg
3 tablespoons butter or margarine

Preheat oven to 375°.

Arrange apple slices in a 9-inch round cake pan. Mix all other ingredients, except butter or margarine, until crumbly and sprinkle over the top.

Drizzle with melted butter. Bake at 375° for 30 minutes or until apples are done.

6 servings

Yogurt Cake Saint-Elie

Readings, vigils and prayer—these are the things that lend stability to the wondering mind.

—*Evagrius Ponticus*

3 cups sifted flour
2 cups sugar
1 teaspoon baking powder (double
   if whole-wheat flour is used)
3 eggs
1 cup natural yogurt*
1 teaspoon vanilla
3/4 cup oil

Preheat oven to 350°.

Butter and flour an 8-inch square cake pan. Combine dry ingredients. Beat eggs thoroughly. Beat in yogurt, vanilla, and oil; add dry ingredients. Pour into baking pan. Bake about 50 minutes at 350°.

NOTE: Avoid yogurts containing stabilizers. If you can get natural yogurt with fruits, etc., they will work; decrease sugar if yogurt is sweetened.

AUTUMN

God, by providence, maintains the world in a state of perpetual change—seasons, light and darkness, rain and sunshine, storm and calm. All this enhances the beauty of creation.

—St. Francis de Sales

Soups

Soup Julienne
(Potage Julienne au bouillon)

A person can show his religion as much in measuring onions as he can in singing "Glory hallelujah!"

—Shaker brother

3 leeks (white part only)
4 carrots
2 medium turnips
1/2 medium green cabbage
1 onion
3 bouillon cubes
3 quarts water
salt and pepper to taste
1/3 cup minced fresh parsley

Cut the vegetables in thin strips, 1 1/2 inches long, and place them in a large soup kettle with the water. Add the bouillon cubes and bring the water to boil. Reduce the heat to medium, cover, and cook the soup slowly for about 45 minutes, stirring from time to time.

When the vegetables are done, add the salt, pepper, and parsley; stir a few times, cover, and simmer for 15 additional minutes. Serve hot.

6 servings

Escarole Soup

Noo spiritual exercises can be compared to that of silence for those who wish to acquire inner peace.

—*St. Seraphim of Sarov*

1 1/2 **pounds escarole, coarsely chopped**
  1 **onion, finely chopped**
  3 **garlic cloves, minced**
  6 **tablespoons olive oil**
  2 **quarts water**
  3 **bouillon cubes**
1/2 **cup vermicelli noodles or any other small pasta**
    salt and ground pepper to taste
    grated cheese of your choice (optional)

Sauté the garlic and onion in the oil in a large kettle for 3 to 4 minutes. Add the escarole and stir so that the oil is evenly distributeed.

Add the water and the bouillon, and cook over medium heat, covered, for 15 minutes. After 15 minutes, add the vermicelli noodles, salt and pepper, and continue cooking for another 10 minutes, stirring occasionally. Turn off the heat, and with the lid in place, allow the soup to rest for an additional 10 minutes before serving. Sprinkle grated cheese on the top of each serving, if you wish.

6 servings

Basic Monastic Garlic Soup

Sing as travelers sing: sing and walk! Not to pamper laziness but to maintain strength. Sing and walk! As you walk, advance in good works, advance in upright faith, advance in a pure life without going astray, without backsliding, without stopping. Sing and walk!

—*St. Augustine*

16 large garlic cloves, minced
4 tablespoons olive oil, (or more)
1 cup dry white wine
6 cups bouillon
  salt to taste
1/4 teaspoon nutmeg
6 slices whole wheat bread
3 egg yolks, beaten
3 egg whites, beaten stiff

Sauté the garlic in olive oil in a soup kettle for a few minutes. Add the wine, bouillon, salt and nutmeg, and bring to boil. Reduce the heat to low to medium, add the egg yolks, and cook for 15 minutes. Simmer for another 15 minutes, covered.

Place one slice of bread in each of six soup plates. Scatter the stiff egg whites over the bread. Ladle the hot soup over the bread and serve immediately.

6 servings

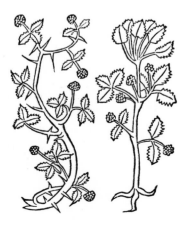

Lentil and Lemon Peel Soup

One must never forget that on the human side a monastic life is the desert; on the spiritual side, the communion of saints in heaven.

—*Mother Maria*

1 cup lentils
6 cups water
1 onion, finely chopped
4 garlic cloves, minced
2 bouillon cubes
4 tablespoons olive oil
  salt and pepper
  peel of 1/2 lemon, grated

Combine all ingredients in a large kettle, and simmer until lentils are tender, about 1 1/2 hours. Stir occasionally and check to see that there is enough liquid to prevent burning. Serve hot.

4–6 servings

Main Dishes

Eggs Cocotte
(Oeufs cocotte)

In the midst of our work we can fulfill the duty of prayer, giving thanks to him who has granted strength to our hands for performing our tasks and cleverness to our minds for acquiring knowledge, and for providing the materials.

—from the Long Rules of St. Basil

1 1/2 **cups heavy cream**
  6 **eggs**
    salt and pepper to taste

Preheat oven to 350°.

Put 2 tablespoons heavy cream in each of six ramekins and place in ovenproof saucepan or skillet. Add water to come half way up the side of the bowls, but do not let the water get inside the bowls.

Boil the water for exactly 2 minutes, and then break an egg into each of the bowls and cover the top with 2 more tablespoonfuls of heavy cream. Sprinkle salt and pepper on each egg and place the entire bain-marie in oven at 350° for about 6 minutes. Serve immediately.

NOTE: This simple dish may be used as an introduction to a good meal or it is a nutritious lunch or light supper by itself.

6 servings

Cauliflower Fritters

The human heart lies open to God alone, for it is a fathomless depth.

—*St. Seraphim of Sarov*

1 head cauliflower
1 egg, beaten lightly
1/2 cup milk
3/4 cup flour
3/4 cup grated cheese of your choice
  pinch of salt
  oil for deep fat frying

Cook the whole cauliflower in lightly salted water in a deep saucepan for 5 to 6 minutes. It should remain firm. Separate the cauliflower into florets, and put in colander to ensure that excess water drains off.

Combine beaten egg, milk, flour, cheese, and a pinch of salt, and beat until creamy and smooth. Let the batter rest for at least an hour before using it. Dip each floret into the batter and fry in hot deep vegetable oil. Serve hot.

4 servings

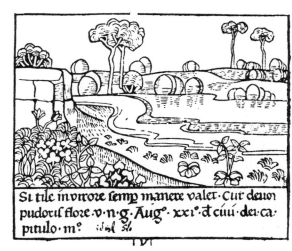

Butternut Squash with Garlic

Work is to be undertaken, not merely for the sake of keeping the body under subjection, but also for showing love to our neighbor, in order that through us God may provide a sufficiency for those brethren who are in want.

—from the Long Rules by St. Basil

5 butternut squashes
4 ounces butter or 1/2 cup vegetable oil
6 large garlic cloves, minced
　 salt and freshly ground pepper to
　 taste
　 finely chopped parsley (optional)

Wash and peel the squash; remove the seeds; cut into 2-inch cubes. Cover with water and boil 5 to 7 minutes, being careful not to overcook. Cubes should remain firm. Drain.

In a large skillet melt the butter or heat oil, add the finely minced garlic cloves and sauté for one minute. Do not allow the garlic to brown or burn.

Place the squash cubes in a serving bowl and pour the melted butter or vegetable oil and garlic over them. Sprinkle with salt and pepper to taste and gently toss the vegetable. Finely chopped parsley makes an attractive garnish. Serve immediately.

4–6 servings

Broccoli with Hollandaise Sauce

Nothing should alienate us from one another, but that which alienates us from God.

—*Benjamin Whichcote*

4 large broccoli stems

hollandaise sauce
1/2 cup melted butter
3 egg yolks
1 tablespoon lemon juice
1/2 teaspoon salt
1/4 teaspoon white pepper
   dash of nutmeg
1/3 cup boiling water

Wash the broccoli stems and cut in four pieces lengthwise. Trim the ends. Cook until the stalks are tender.

Meanwhile, prepare a hollandaise sauce in the top of a double boiler by whisking the melted butter and adding one egg yolk at a time. Add lemon juice, salt, pepper, and nutmeg while continuing to whisk. Just before serving, place over boiling water and add, little by little, 1/3 cup of boiling water to the sauce, constantly stirring, until the sauce thickens. To prevent further cooking, separate pan with sauce from lower part of double boiler.

Drain the broccoli, salt to taste, and serve with the hollandaise sauce.

4 servings

Saint Hubert Fish Stew

Then only is our life a whole, when work and contemplation dwell in us side by side, and we are perfectly in both of them at once.

—*Ruysbroeck*

2 onions, chopped
4 garlic cloves, minced
6 tablespoons vegetable oil
1 pound cod or similar fish
4 carrots, sliced
2 parsnips, sliced
3 potatoes, diced
4 tablespoons chopped parsley
1 bay leaf
2 bottles beer
4 cups water
   salt and white pepper to taste

Sauté the onion and garlic in the oil in a stew pot for a few minutes.

Add the remaining ingredients, stir well, cover, and cook slowly over low to medium heat for 35 to 40 minutes. Stir from time to time so that the stew does not burn at the bottom. Serve hot.

6 servings

Lentils and Potatoes with Pesto Sauce

Put your hands to work, and your hearts to God, and a blessing will attend you.

—*Mother Ann Lee, Shaker sister*

2 cups dried lentils
4 potatoes, cubed

pesto sauce
2 cups chopped fresh basil
6 garlic cloves, minced
1/2 cup olive oil
a few sprigs of parsley and thyme
salt and ground pepper to taste

Preheat oven to 350°.

Wash and drain the lentils. Boil them until they are tender. Drain.

Meanwhile, boil the potatoes in a separate saucepan. They must remain firm and not overcooked. Drain.

Blend the pesto ingredients in a food processor or blender until smooth (add more oil if necessary).

Thoroughly butter a deep baking dish. Place the lentils and potatoes in it. Add the pesto sauce and mix well. Bake at 350° for about 20 minutes. Serve hot.

6 servings

Ragout of the Harvest

He who sees things grow from the beginning will have the best view of them.

—*Aristotle*

1 onion, chopped
6 tomatoes, peeled and sliced
4 garlic cloves, minced
1/3 cup mixed fresh herbs, chopped
and minced (parsley, basil,
thyme)
1 bay leaf
1 cup white wine or vermouth
6 potatoes, sliced
4 carrots, sliced
1/2 pound lima beans (or 1 package,
frozen)
1 zucchini or yellow squash, sliced
olive oil
salt and pepper to taste

Gently sauté the onions in a large saucepan until they begin to turn golden. Add the tomatoes, the minced garlic, the herbs, and the bay leaf and cook for about 5 minutes, stirring from time to time.

Stir in the cup of wine or vermouth, and cook a minute or two. Add the potatoes, carrots, and lima beans. Cover the pan and cook over low or medium heat until the vegetables are tender. Add the zucchini or squash, and continue cooking for another 8 minutes. Season to taste and add more wine if needed. When the ragout is ready, it should rest with the lid on for at least 5 minutes before serving. Serve hot.

NOTE: This vegetable stew is a special treat at harvest time when the abundance of the garden can easily be transplanted to the table.

4–6 servings

Soybean Casserole

The grand essentials to happiness in this life are something to do, something to love, and something to hope for.

—*Joseph Addison*

 1 cup dried soybeans
 2 onions, sliced
 2 garlic cloves, minced
 1 carrot, sliced
 1 celery stalk, sliced fine
 1 cup chopped spinach
 1/2 cup chopped parsley
 10 ounces tofu, cut in cubes
 4 tablespoons vegetable oil
 2 tablespoons soy sauce
   salt and pepper to taste
   grated cheese of your choice

Preheat oven to 300°.

Rinse the beans and soak in water. Drain. Cover the beans with fresh water and bring to boil. Skim off the foam that forms on top of the water and reduce the heat. With the saucepan covered, cook the beans for about 1 hour 45 minutes, or at least until the beans are soft and tender. Stir from time to time so that the beans do not burn at the bottom.

Thoroughly butter a large baking dish that has a cover. Place the beans and all the other ingredients, except the cheese, in the dish. Add one cup water and mix well. Cover the dish and bake at 300° for about 1 hour. Uncover the dish, sprinkle on the grated cheese, and return to the oven for about 5 minutes until the cheese melts. Serve hot.

4–6 servings

Zucchini Loaf

Establish yourself in God and then you will be helpful to others.

—*St. Seraphim of Sarov*

4 medium zucchinis, sliced
1 large onion, diced
1 green pepper, diced
1 sweet red pepper, diced
4 garlic cloves, minced
  minced herbs (fresh parsley, thyme, basil)
2 eggs
1/3 cup milk
8 slices whole wheat bread
2 eggs, hard-boiled and mashed
  salt and pepper to taste
  olive oil

Preheat oven to 350°.

Gently sauté the sliced zucchinis, onion, and peppers in olive oil in a large skillet. Remove from heat, add the minced garlic and herbs, and then cover the skillet.

In a large deep bowl beat the 2 eggs and the milk together thoroughly. Add salt and pepper and continue beating. Slowly crumble the bread slices into the bowl, add the well-mashed hard-boiled eggs and the vegetables. With greased hands, mix and blend the contents of the bowl thoroughly and form into a large round ball. Refrigerate it in the bowl for at least 2 hours.

Press the zucchini loaf into a well-buttered pan. Bake at 350° for 25 to 30 minutes. Remove from the pan immediately.

NOTE: This attractive and easy-to-prepare vegetarian dish may be served either hot or cold.

6–8 servings

Spicy Rice-Vegetable Casserole

Whatever a man possess over and above what is necessary for life, he is obliged to do good with, according to the command of the Lord who has bestowed on us the things we possess.

—from the Short Rules of St. Basil

3 tablespoons butter
1/2 green pepper, chopped
1 onion, chopped
2 garlic cloves, mashed
1 1/2 cups rice (uncooked)
3 carrots, sliced
3 large stalks celery, sliced
1/2 teaspoon thyme
1/2 teaspoon oregano (adjust to your taste)
salt and pepper
1 cup canned chick peas, drained (optional)

Preheat oven to 350°.

In an oven proof dish with a lid, melt butter; stir in rice so that all grains are coated. Add remaining ingredients and mix thoroughly.

Stir in 3 1/2 cups boiling water. Cover. Bake at 350° for 1 hour. You may wish to add 1 cup of heated chick peas during the last 10 minutes.

6–8 servings

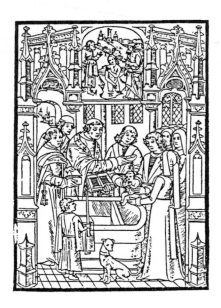

Risotto
(seasoned rice)

Mutual forgiveness of each vice
Open the gates of paradise.

—*William Blake*

1 onion
1 carrot
2 stalks celery
1 1/2 cups rice
    salt to taste
2–2 1/2 cups broth or bouillon
2 teaspoons thyme
1/2 cup white wine
    grated cheese (Parmesan is best)

In a large frying pan, gently sauté finely chopped onion, carrot, and celery in a little cooking oil. Add rice, 2 cups broth, and thyme.

Cook over medium heat. When the mixture begins to stick to the pan, add the wine. Continue cooking until the rice is tender. The mixture will dry out as it cooks, so keep adding broth or bouillon to maintain moistness. If the rice is a variety which cooks quickly, you may have some broth left over. If, however, you use brown rice or another longer-cooking variety, you may have to add more broth or bouillon. Stir only to prevent sticking and when adding liquid. Otherwise, let simmer.

Sprinkle with grated cheese just before serving in a covered bowl which has been previously warmed.

6 servings

Indian Curried Lentils

Love a man even in his sin, for that is the semblance of divine love and is the highest love on earth.

—*Fyodor Dostoevsky*

1 pound dried lentils
1 cinnamon stick
  few peppercorns
2 onions, sliced
1 tablespoon curry powder
3 1/2 cups canned whole tomatoes
4 tablespoons margarine
  salt to taste
  eggs, hard-boiled (optional)
  shrimp, cooked (optional)

In a kettle, cover lentils with water and boil with cinnamon stick and peppercorns until lentils are tender. Drain and remove peppercorns and cinnamon stick.

Sauté onions in margarine and then add other ingredients. Stir and heat through. Two quartered hard-boiled eggs or cooked shrimp may be added. Serve hot.

4 servings

Hudson Valley Codfish Cakes

Solitude and prayer are the greatest means to acquire virtues. Purifying the mind, they make it possible to see the unseen.

—*St. Seraphim of Sarov*

4 cups flaked codfish
7–8 medium potatoes
1/2–3/4 cup scalded milk
2 eggs, well beaten
1 medium onion, grated
salt and pepper to taste

Cover fish with cold water and bring to a boil; drain.

Cook potatoes and mash. Add scalded milk and beat well. Add eggs and onion and continue beating until mixture is creamy. Stir in flaked fish. Form into balls, press flat, and fry lightly on each side.

16–20 small cakes

Eggplant Omelette

And when we find ourselves in the place just right, it will be in the valley of love and delight.

—*Shaker Hymn*

1 small eggplant, thinly sliced
3 garlic cloves, minced
1 large onion, sliced
6 eggs
1 teaspoon cornstarch
1/2 cup milk
   salt and pepper to taste
   oil

In a large frying pan, fry eggplant, garlic, and onion gently in oil until they are cooked (about 5 to 10 minutes).

Beat the eggs.

Make a paste by mixing cornstarch and a little milk; add remaining milk, and mix well with the eggs and seasonings.

Pour egg-milk mixture over the cooked eggplant and cook as an omelette. Serve immediately.

4 servings

Roman Gnocchi
(Gnocchis à la Romaine)

We are meant to believe through all darkness that God is love and only love, and to try to live by that faith alone.

—*Mother Maria*

2 cups milk
dash nutmeg, salt
3/4 cup farina
2 eggs plus 1 yolk, beaten slightly
2 tablespoons butter
1 cup grated cheese, Italian preferred

Preheat oven to 425°.

Scald milk with nutmeg and salt. When just at boiling point, sprinkle in farina while stirring. Keep stirring as farina thickens. Turn off heat and beat in eggs, then 1/2 cup cheese.

Pour into an 8-inch square pan and smooth surface so thickness is even. Chill thoroughly.

Cut the cold gnocchi into squares, diamonds, etc. Place on an ovenproof, buttered platter. Dot butter on top; sprinkle with cheese. Bake at 425° for 10 to 15 minutes.

4 servings

Salads

Kasha Salad

Love God's young creation, love it as a whole and every grain of sand in it. Love every leaf, every ray of God. Love animals, love every plant and everything. If you love every thing, the mystery of God will be revealed to you in things . . . . And finally you will love the whole universe with a comprehensive, all-embracing love.

—*Fyodor Dostoevsky*

 4 ounces kasha
 2 stalks celery, finely chopped
 1 green pepper, diced
 1 red pepper, diced
 4 medium tomatoes, chopped
 1 medium onion, chopped
 1/3 cup finely chopped fresh parsley
 6 tablespoons olive oil (add more according to taste)
 2 tablespoons lemon juice
 salt and pepper to taste

Cover kasha with boiling water in a large saucepan. Simmer for 10 to 15 minutes, covered. Drain thoroughly and refrigerate the kasha for 1 hour.

Place the kasha with the diced and chopped ingredients in a deep salad bowl and mix thoroughly. Combine the olive oil with lemon juice and pour over. Toss. Adjust seasoning. Serve cold.

NOTE: This nutritious and pleasant salad is good any time of year, but especially when tomatoes are ripe and sweet.

4–6 servings

String Bean Salad

Prayer is the outcome of love, it is a form of love, it is therefore creative since love is the very life of God himself. The nearer anyone draws to God, the nearer he draws to all that God loves, that is, to the whole world and every single person in it.

—*Sister Thekla*

1 **pound string beans**
1 **red onion, thinly sliced**
1/3 **cup finely chopped fresh parsley**
    leaf lettuce

vinaigrette
8 **tablespoons olive oil**
2 **tablespoons white vermouth**
2 **tablespoons lemon juice**
    salt and pepper to taste
    egg, hard-boiled and sliced
    (optional)

Wash and trim the string beans, and if they are especially long, cut them in half. Cook for 15 minutes in boiling water and then rinse them with cold water. Drain thoroughly.

Add the onion and parsley. Prepare the vinaigrette according to directions in The Basics section; pour over the salad and mix well.

Arrange lettuce on individual plates with the string beans on the top. Garnish with slices of hard-boiled eggs, if desired.

6–8 servings

Desserts

Pudding Délice

Though the saint knows the mountain of God's love from having lived on its heights, the pilgrim in the valley can at least see the mountain and appreciate its grandeur from the distance. He or she can call out to other pilgrims and tell them of life lived on the heights.

—*Peter Kreeft*

1/3 cup butter
1/4 teaspoon salt
1 cup sugar
2 eggs
1 tablespoon vanilla extract or cognac
1 1/3 cup sifted flour
3 teaspoons baking powder
1/2 cup milk

Cream the butter, salt, and sugar. Add the eggs and vanilla or cognac. Beat well. Add the flour and baking powder alternately with the milk and continue beating.

Pour the mixture into a buttered casserole dish and bake at 350° for 35 to 40 minutes until the pudding sets. Allow to cool and cut in squares. Serve with fruit and whipped cream.

4–6 servings

Saint Bruno's Coffee Cream

(Crème au café Saint Bruno)

Saint Bruno was the founder of the order of Carthusian monks in the 11th century. Born in Cologne, he taught theology at the Rheims cathedral school. Later he withdrew with six companions to the wilderness of the Grande Chartreuse. There he built hermitages and established the Carthusian monastic way of life which combines solitary and communal life. In a letter to an old friend, he spoke of the great beauty of that way of life: "Only those who experience it can know the benefit and delight to be had from the quietness and solitude of a hermitage."

1 quart milk
2 tablespoons instant coffee
2 teaspoons coffee extract or coffee liqueur
6 egg yolks, well beaten
1/2 cup sugar

In a heavy saucepan combine the milk, instant coffee, and coffee extract or coffee liqueur. Bring almost to boil while stirring constantly.

Combine egg yolks and sugar in a mixing bowl; beat thoroughly. Slowly, pour the hot milk into the egg mixture while continuing to beat with the mixer. It must be thoroughly blended.

Return the mixture to the saucepan and cook over low to medium heat, stirring continually until the cream begins to thicken. Just before the mixture reaches the boiling point, remove from heat and pour into bowl. Stir once or twice, cover, and refrigerate until serving time.

4–6 servings

Peaches with Strawberries "Monte Cassino"

(Pêches aux fraises Mont Cassin)

Monks should practice zeal with ardent love. They should anticipate one another in honor, most patiently endure one another's infirmities, whether of body or soul. Let them try to outdo each other in obedience. Let no one do what is best for himself, but rather what is best for another.

—*from the Holy Rule of St. Benedict*

10 ounces strawberries
3 pounds peaches
4 tablespoons strawberry jam
1 cup fruity white wine
1 cup sugar

Wash and trim the strawberries. Dip the peaches in boiling water, cool, and carefully peel and cut in perfect halves. Pit. Refrigerate with the strawberries.

Combine the jam, wine, and sugar in a heavy saucepan. Simmer over low heat stirring constantly until sugar dissolves and mixture thickens into a syrup. Cool.

When it is time to serve the dessert, slice strawberries. Place peach halves on dessert plates, fill hollows with sliced strawberries, and pour the syrup on top.

6–8 servings

Cold Spring Rice Pudding
(Riz aux oeufs)

God wants us to sing alleluia and to sing it truthfully from our hearts without any sour notes from the singer. Let us sing alleluia with our voice and our heart, with our mouth and with our life.

—*St. Augustine*

1 cup rice
1 cup boiling water
3 cups milk
3 eggs
1/2 cup sugar
1 teaspoon vanilla
pinch of nutmeg
1/2–1 cup raisins (optional)
1 teaspoon cinnamon (optional)

Preheat oven to 350°.

Combine rice and boiling water. Cover and let sit 40 minutes or until water is absorbed. (Rice will be partially cooked.)

Beat together all other ingredients. Put rice in a deep buttered baking dish; pour egg mixture over it. Bake for 50 minutes at 350° or until custard is set.

8 servings

Saint Placid's Pumpkin Chiffon Pie

Saint Gregory's *Dialogues* charmingly narrates how Placid became one of St. Benedict's first disciples in Monte Cassino and how he was saved from drowning by the prayers of the Holy Patriarch. St. Benedict had a particular affection for the young Placid, since the child was entrusted to the care of St. Benedict. St. Placid's feast was celebrated until recently on the 5th of October, hence his name on a harvest dish.

1 cup sugar
1/2 cup milk
2 cups canned pumpkin
3 egg yolks, well beaten
1/3 tablespoon salt
2 teaspoons cinnamon
1 teaspoon vanilla extract
1 envelope plain gelatin
1/4 cup cold water
3 egg whites, beaten stiff

pastry shell
2 cups flour
1 stick sweet butter
1 egg
5 tablespoons ice water
pinch salt

Prepare the pastry shell according to the instructions in The Basics section. Bake until done and allow to cool.

Combine the sugar, milk, pumpkin, egg yolks, salt, cinnamon, and vanilla in a saucepan. Cook slowly over low heat, stirring constantly and mashing any lumps until the mixture thickens and becomes smooth.

In a large bowl, soften the gelatin in the cold water. Slowly add the pumpkin mixture, stirring constantly. Set the bowl in ice water to cool. When the mixture is cool and begins to congeal, fold in beaten egg whites. Pour the pumpkin mixture into the baked pie shell and chill for at least 4 hours.

Quick Apple Cake
(Gateau aux pommes)

As we progress in our monastic life and faith, our hearts expand and we run the way of God's commandments with unspeakable sweetness of love. Thus, never departing from his school, but persevering in the monastery until death, we may by patience share in the passion of Christ and deserve to have a share also in his kingdom.

—from the Holy Rule of St. Benedict

2 eggs
1/3 cup milk
2 teaspoons baking powder
6 tablespoons sugar (white or light brown)
3/4 cup whole wheat flour
small pinch salt
1/3 cup oil
4 apples, peeled, cored, cut in 1/4-inch slices
1/2 cup cream or condensed milk
1 teaspoon cinnamon

Preheat oven to 350°.

Butter an 8-inch baking pan. Beat eggs well; add milk. Combine dry ingredients, except cinnamon, and add to egg mixture; beat in oil. Batter should be quite thick.

Spread batter in pan. Arrange the apple slices on edge over entire surface. Bake 15 minutes. Remove from oven, and pour cream or condensed milk over surface and sprinkle with cinnamon. Return to oven for another 25 minutes.

THE BASICS

Basic Sauces for Hot Dishes

Sauce Béchamel

2 tablespoons butter or margarine
2 tablespoons corn starch or flour
2 cups milk
1 tablespoon dry sherry (optional)
  salt and white pepper to taste
  pinch of nutmeg (optional)

Melt butter or margarine in a stainless steel pan over low to medium heat. Add the corn starch or flour and stir with a whisk. Add the milk, little by little, until smooth, continuing to whisk. Add the sherry, salt, pepper, nutmeg, and continue stirring. When it begins to boil, reduce the heat, and cook slowly until it thickens.

This sauce is excellent for use with fish, vegetables, and a necessary base for soufflés, some omelettes, and other egg dishes.

Sauce Mornay

2 cups of Béchamel sauce (see preceding recipe)
4 tablespoons Romano or Parmesan cheese
4 tablespoons grated Gruyère cheese
10 tablespoons heavy cream

When the Béchamel sauce is at boiling point, add the cheese and let it melt as the sauce thickens. When the sauce is smooth and thick, withdraw from the heat, and add the heavy cream while stirring continually with a whisk or a mixer.

White Sauce

2 tablespoons butter or margarine
2 teaspoons corn starch or flour
1 1/2 cup milk
  salt and freshly ground black pepper
  nutmeg (optional)

Dissolve the corn starch or flour in 1/2 cup milk. Melt the butter or margarine in a stainless steel pan over medium heat. When it begins foaming, add the milk mixture, stirring continually. Add the rest of the milk, salt and pepper, nutmeg, and stir until the sauce comes to a boiling point. Lower the heat and continue stirring until the sauce thickens. The sauce is ready when it is smooth and thick.

This sauce can be used as a basis for many other useful variations. It can be used on fish, meats, eggs, and vegetables.

White Sauce with Mustard

Prepare a white sauce, and stir in 1 teaspoon of French or dry mustard.

White Sauce with Herbs

Prepare a white sauce. Add 3 tablespoons of finely chopped fresh herbs (tarragon, dill, parsley, thyme, etc.) and 1/2 teaspoon dry mustard. Mix thoroughly.

Hollandaise Sauce

1/2 cup melted butter
 3 egg yolks
 1 tablespoon fresh lemon juice
1/2 teaspoon salt
1/4 teaspoon white pepper
    dash of nutmeg
1/3 cup boiling water

Whisk the melted butter with a mixer while adding one egg yolk at a time. Add the lemon juice, salt and pepper, and nutmeg, continuing to whisk with the mixer. Just before serving, place the bowl in a saucepan with 1 inch boiling water, or in the upper part of a double boiler. Over low heat add, little by little, 1/3 cup of boiling water to the sauce while stirring continuously until the sauce thickens.

This sauce can be used on fish, veal, egg and vegetable dishes.

Tomato Sauce

 6 tablespoons olive oil
 1 large onion, finely chopped
 3 garlic cloves, minced
 2 pounds tomatoes, skinned and sliced
 3 tablespoons tomato purée
 1 carrot, grated
 4 tablespoons fresh basil, finely chopped
 1 bay leaf
    salt and pepper to taste
    pinch of thyme

Heat the olive oil in an enamel or stainless steel saucepan and sauté the onion and the garlic slowly for a few minutes until they are soft and transparent. Add the rest of the ingredients. Lower the heat and simmer for 30 to 40 minutes, stirring from time to time. While the sauce is cooking, partially cover the saucepan. When cooking time is complete, turn the heat off and let the sauce rest a few minutes before serving. Good on pasta dishes and egg dishes.

Pesto Sauce

(Sauce au pistou)

 4 garlic cloves, minced
1/2 cup fresh basil leaves, finely chopped
1/3 cup pistachio nuts, finely chopped
 6 tablespoons grated Parmesan cheese
 1 cup olive oil (or more)
    a pinch of salt

Mash the garlic and basil with a mortar and pestle. Add the pistachio nuts and continue mashing thoroughly. Place the mixture in a larger container, gradually add the olive oil, cheese, salt, and blend thoroughly.

A simpler and quicker way to prepare the pesto sauce is to place all the ingredients in a blender and process as smooth as you wish.

This sauce is usually used with pasta, but it can also be used with gnocchi, seafood, eggs, and vegetables like zucchini.

Mushroom Sauce

 1 ounce butter or margarine
 1 onion, finely chopped
1/2 pound mushrooms, chopped
 1 cup sherry or white wine
1/2 teaspoon ground turmeric
1/2 cup fresh parsley, finely chopped
    salt and freshly ground pepper

Melt the butter or margarine in an enamel or stainless steel saucepan. Add the onion and cook until transparent. Add the mushrooms, wine, turmeric, salt and pepper, and cook until the mushrooms begin to turn brown. Reduce the heat, add the parsley, and while stirring, cook thoroughly for another 4 to 5 minutes until the sauce is done.

This sauce is excellent on the top of rice, fish, meat, and eggs.

Basic Sauces for Cold Dishes

Simple Vinaigrette

(Vinaigrette classique)

1 teaspoon salt
1/2 teaspoon freshly ground pepper
2 tablespoons wine vinegar
6 tablespoons olive oil

Place the salt and pepper in a cup or bowl. Add the vinegar and stir thoroughly. Add the oil and stir until all the ingredients are completely blended.

Vinaigrette with Herbs

(Vinaigrette aux herbes)

Prepare a simple vinaigrette, but replace the vinegar with equivalent lemon juice. Add 1/4 cup finely chopped herbs (parsley, tarragon, coriander, scallions). Mix thoroughly.

Vinaigrette with Mustard

(Vinaigrette à la moutarde)

Prepare a simple vinaigrette, adding 1 teaspoon French mustard.

Vinaigrette with Garlic

(Vinaigrette à l'ail)

Prepare a simple vinaigrette, adding 1 minced garlic clove. Let the vinaigrette stand for a few hours before using.

Sauce Mayonnaise

1 egg yolk
1 teaspoon mustard
2 teaspoon lemon juice or tarragon vinegar
1 teaspoon salt
1/2 teaspoon white pepper
3/4 cup light olive or vegetable oil

Place the egg yolk in a bowl, add the mustard, salt and pepper, and begin to mix with a whisk or a mixer. Add the oil a little at a time, then lemon juice, or tarragon vinegar, and more oil, continuing to mix until the mayonnaise thickens. Keep the mayonnaise in the refrigerator until it is ready to be used.

The mayonnaise can be used for hard boiled eggs, potato salad, Russian salad, or on asparagus, etc.

Sauce Aioli

Prepare a mayonnaise sauce as indicated above. Add 5 minced garlic cloves. Mix thoroughly and refrigerate the sauce for several hours before using it. This sauce can be used on seafood, salads, vegetables and cold meats.

Tarragon Sauce

(Sauce à l'estragon)

1/2 cup sour cream
3 tablespoons lemon juice
1/2 cup heavy cream
    salt and white pepper to taste
3 tablespoons chopped tarragon

Place all the above ingredients in a deep bowl and with a mixer stir and blend thoroughly. Refrigerate until time to use on salads, seafood, etc.

Pastry

Fine Dough for Tarts and Quiches

(La pâte brisée)

2 cups flour
1 stick butter or margarine
  pinch of salt
1 egg or 2 yolks
5 tablespoons ice water

Preheat oven to 300°.

Work the flour, salt and butter or margarine together with the fingers by rubbing lightly. When texture is even, pour egg and water into well in the center. Using a finger, stir the liquid quickly into the flour, starting at the inside and gradually moving to the outside. Gather the dough up into a ball. Cover with a well-wrung out damp cloth, or with foil, and put in the refrigerator to rest for 1 or more hours.

When the dough is ready to be worked, sprinkle some flour over the table (or board) and carefully roll out the dough, extending it in every direction. Butter a tart or pie dish thoroughly and place the rolled dough into it with care. The dough must always be handled with the fingers. Trim the edges in a decorative fashion. Cover the pastry shell with aluminum foil and place in the oven for 12 to 15 minutes for a pre-baking period. Refer to individual recipe for remaining baking instructions.

This recipe is basically to be used for salty dishes; quiches, vegetable or meat tarts.

Sweet Fine Dough for Fruit Tarts and Pies

(La pate brisée sucrée)

Prepare a basic dough for tarts and quiches, substituting 1 stick of sweet butter for the salty butter, and a pinch of sugar for the salt. You may also add an extra egg for a richer pie crust.

This recipe can be used for dessert dishes; fruit tarts and pies.

Rich Pastry Dough

(a crunchy dessert shell)

2 tablespoons pecans, finely mashed
2 cups whole wheat flour
1 teaspoon baking powder
1 stick sweet butter or margarine
1 teaspoon brown sugar
1 tablespoon vegetable oil
8 tablespoons ice water (more if needed)
  pinch of salt

Prepare the pastry shell by mixing all the ingredients and following the instructions given above for fine dough. The combination of whole wheat flour and nuts provides a splendid rich texture to the crust and gives a nut flavor to tarts and pies.

This crust is excellent for open tarts and pies.

Beverages

Three Kings Brandy Egg Nog

1 egg yolk
1/2 cup cognac
4 tablespoons sugar
4 cups milk
dash of nutmeg

Combine all the ingredients in a blender and process until foamy. Refrigerate if not served immediately.

4 glasses

Honey and Molasses Drink

2 tablespoons honey
2 tablespoons molasses
1 cup water
1 cup milk
dash of nutmeg

Combine the honey, molasses and water in a saucepan. Bring to a boil. Add the milk and nutmeg, continuing to stir. Simmer for 2 or 3 minutes. Serve hot.

2 glasses

Mint Tea

6 tablespoons mint leaves, chopped
4 1/2 cups water
2 inches orange peel

Bring the water to boil and add the mint and orange peel; boil for 5 minutes. Simmer for 2 or 3 minutes more. Strain and serve the tea and let each individual add sugar or honey according to taste.

4 cups

Hot Chocolate
(Chocolat chaud)

2 tablespoons bitter chocolate
1 cup water
1 cup milk
2 tablespoons sugar

Bring the water to boil. Add the chocolate and the sugar. Stir until they are totally dissolved. Add the milk and bring to a simmer. Simmer for 2 or 3 minutes. Serve hot.

2 cups

Coffee, Vienna Style

2 egg yolks
4 teaspoons sugar
2 cups hot coffee (instant is fine)
2 tablespoons heavy cream

Beat each egg yolk in the cup in which the coffee will be served. Add the sugar and mix thoroughly. Pour the hot coffee into each cup and stir. Add 1 tablespoon heavy cream to each cup. Stir and serve immediately.

2 cups

Linden Tea
(Tilleul)

8 linden leaves, including young sprigs and flowers
5 cups water

Bring the water to boil, add the linden leaves and sprigs. Boil for 5 to 8 minutes. Simmer for 2 or 3 minutes. Strain and serve the tea. Let each individual add sugar or honey according to taste.

4 cups

Sodium-Free Herb and Spice Blends

These seasoning mixes are made with dried herbs and spices. If you wish to use herbs from your garden, dry them by hanging in bunches in an airy clean space, out of the sun. When crisp to the touch, crumble the herbs with your fingers, discarding the stems. Measure the ingredients for an herb blend into a bowl and rub together with fingers to mix. Store in airtight containers out of the light.

Bouquet Provençale

(for vegetables, sauces, meats)

1 teaspoon thyme
1 teaspoon basil
1/2 teaspoon rosemary
1/2 teaspoon sage
1 bay leaf (use whole, remove before serving food)

Prunelle de Mes Yeux

(for vegetables, meat, grains)

1 teaspoon dry mustard
1/2 teaspoon sage
1/2 teaspoon thyme
1/2 teaspoon white pepper
1 teaspoon chives

Mes Épices

(for vegetables, seafood, sauces)

3/4 teaspoon parsley flakes
1/2 teaspoon onion powder
1 teaspoon sweet red pepper
1 teaspoon tarragon
1/4 teaspoon paprika
1/2 teaspoon lemon flakes

Herbes Melangées

(for vegetables, sauces, poultry)

1/2 teaspoon garlic powder
1/2 teaspoon marjoram
1/2 teaspoon thyme
1/2 teaspoon oregano
1/2 teaspoon sage
1/2 teaspoon chives

Useful Tips for a Healthier Diet

1. Use herbs and spices as salt substitutes.
2. Use more low-fat and skim milk than regular milk.
3. Many main courses can be served with light rather than rich sauces.
4. Sauté with olive oil or margarine rather than butter.
5. Eat fresh whole-wheat and whole-grain breads instead of white bread.
6. Cook with fresh vegetables rather than canned or frozen ones.
7. Be aware of portion sizes and nutrition content of foods.
8. Serve fruit for dessert.